Ocean House

York Beach, Maine

FRED MERRIAM

 www.trafford.com

North America & international
toll-free: 1 888 232 4444 (USA & Canada)
fax: 812 355 4082

ACKNOWLEDGEMENTS

This project was started with encouragement from my wife Carol, who had collected an album of vintage York Beach postcards on eBay. Casual conversations with Betsy Camp, Richard Bucknam, and Phil Meader in the parking lot next door to Ocean House revealed that there were myths and unanswered questions surrounding the origins and timeline of the Ocean House hotel, motel, and outbuildings.

Friday trips to the York County Registry of Deeds in Alfred, Maine, on cold winter days yielded an accurate timeline starting with Ellis family land purchases in 1882 and continuing through the present. Documents and plans acquired at the Registry of Deeds are credited by book number and page number in the format: Book#/Page#

The Museums of Old York has an extensive collection of historical books, maps, postcards, and photographs. Archivist Nancy Moran and Curator Cynthia Young-Gomes were particularly helpful in locating information and photos relating to the Ellis family years at Ocean House.

The Special Collections Department in the library at the University of Maine, Orono had a copy of Fred Ellis's c.1903 Ocean House promotional brochure. Thanks go to Desiree Butterfield-Nagy who scanned this document and made it available.

Betsy Camp, whose grandfather and father operated Ocean House from 1932 to 1976, was very generous with her archives which included family photos, on-the-job photos, and newspaper articles from the Camp, Rivers, and Dunfey eras. She also wrote a firsthand account of her experiences as an employee from 1961 to 1976.

Phil Meader, a volunteer firefighter during the Ocen House condominium fire of March 20, 1986, lent his personal collection of memorabilia and photos.

David Pahl took extensive photographs of Ocean House during the hotel demolition, condominium construction, and condominium fire. After his death in January 2014, his Ocean House photo album was given by his son to Betsy Camp, who made it available for this project.

Peter Stanley, who worked at the Ocean House from 1964 to 1970, wrote down some of his memories of that time.

Several people provided information and support by telephone; Bill Burnham, Fred Manzi, Dennis Reid, Ginny Spiller, and David Stormont.

Thanks go to the following people for proofreading the initial draft of the book; Betsy Camp, John and Sandra Hopkins, and Carol Merriam. For final proofreading; Betsy Camp, Sandra Hopkins, and Ron Nowell.

Short Sands Beach and Concordville from Union Bluff, c.1875. (Museums of Old York)

TABLE OF CONTENTS

INTRODUCTION

". . . Spring Greetings to All Friends . . . Summer memories! Happy days with easy informality at the seashore: sandy beaches, flying surf, rocky cliffs, sheltered coves. Weiner roasts, hiking to the Nubble, shuffleboard tournaments, the golden social hour before sunset and best of all, congenial people with whom to enjoy all.

"Since 1883 Ocean House, with its annex and cottages, has rested like a crown on the crest of a dune with a sweeping view of the majestic Atlantic and the rugged headlands which protect 'Short Sands . . .'"

(Excerpt from the Ocean House flyer for 1956)

Hazen Ellis and his wife, Ellen, rode the wave of prosperity that followed the Civil War developing land in Vineland, New Jersey. In 1883 they saw an opportunity to showcase their four musically talented children and apply their construction and land development skills in York Beach, Maine. Their efforts to sell small subdivision lots on Union Bluff apparently didn't take off, but what they did with a large expanse of sandy scrub land purchased in bits and pieces from several local landowners is the story of York Beach itself.

Ocean House c. 1886 (Phil Meader)

Ellis Family Ownership

The Early Years

August 12, 1849, Hazen Zachary Ellis age 24 married Ellen Naomi Boynton age 18 in Boston, Massachusetts. At this time, Hazen was doing business in the old Faneuil Hall market. In 1851 he sold out and established a general merchandise business in Amherst, NH. From there, they went south and settled in Arkansas, where they engaged in cotton raising. A daughter, Romie M. Ellis, was born on November 24, 1855 in Little Rock. After that they became the proprietors of the St. Charles hotel in Fort Smith, and still later the Van Buren house in Van Buren, Arkansas.

Returning to New England before the outbreak of the Civil War they took up residence in Vermont where Hazen built a large store at Hyde Park (just north of Montpelier) and again ran a general merchandise business. Twin sons Fred A. and Frank H. Ellis were born in Hyde Park on June 7, 1860.

In 1862, to escape the harsh winters of Vermont, along with his brother Stephen T. Ellis, Hazen relocated his family to the milder climate of Vineland, New Jersey (about 33 miles west of Atlantic City). Hazen was attracted to this region by a publication called the *Vineland Rural* and became active in the development of this much advertised health resort and fruit bearing region, selling thousands of acres of land and establishing and editing the *Vineland Advertiser*. Another daughter, Fannie M. Ellis, was born on May 25, 1869, in Vineland. In 1882 the family started purchasing land on Union Bluff in York, Maine.

Known as the Ellis Family Bell Ringers, they came to York Beach as entertainers. Romie, Fannie, Frank and Fred performed with 60 silver hand bells, a staff of tuned sleigh bells, a staff of silver bells with hammer, a set of cut glass goblets played with wet fingers, and

Romie, Fannie, and twins Frank and Fred Ellis c. 1884. (Museums of Old York)

accompanied by guitar. Fannie also played the German zither.

(References: Ancestry.com, the *Vineland Historical Magazine*, and the February 28, 1902 issue of *The York Courant and Transcript* from the Museums of Old York)

1882

- *November 28,* Oldest daughter Romie Ellis, whose residence was listed as Newark, New Jersey, purchased a 110 x 36 foot ocean front lot on Union Bluff for $150 from Harrison F. Wood of Dover, NH. [388/368]

This was the first of many Ellis family land purchases in York.

1883

During this year the family wintered in Springfield, Massachusetts and Philadelphia, Pennsylvania but made purchases of land on the Union Bluff in York, Maine throughout the year.

- *January 8,* Ellen, Fred, Frank, and Fannie Ellis purchased four 110 x 36 foot ocean front lots on Union Bluff for $100 each from Nathaniel Shattuck and George Davis. [388/445, 388/446, 388/447, 388/449]

- *January 9,* Ellen, Fred, Frank, and Fannie Ellis purchased from Nicholas Meade for $1 his interest in the four lots on Union Bluff they had purchased the day before from Nathaniel Shattuck and George Davis. [388/450]

- *July 18,* Ellen Ellis purchased a 200 x 40 foot ocean front lot on Union Bluff from Nathaniel Shattuck for $100. [392/368]

- *August 3,* Ellen Ellis purchased two parcels of land on Union Bluff (one a pasture and the other ocean front) from John Richardson and Edgar Freeman for $400 each. [394/197, 395/40]

- *August 5,* Ellen, Romie, Frank, and Fred Ellis purchased subdivision lots 3, 4, and 5 on Union Bluff from George Davis and Nicholas Meade for $25. [392/468]

- *August 6,* Frank and Fred Ellis purchased a 225 x 40 foot ocean front lot on Union Bluff with buildings thereon from Charles H. Perrin. [392/438]

- *September 18,* Hazen Ellis purchased subdivision lots 13 through 18 on Union Bluff from Nathaniel Shattuck for $650. [392/532]

- *October 25,* Ellen Ellis purchased an ocean front lot on Union Bluff from George Varney for $15. [399/20]

- *December 28,* Ellen Ellis purchased subdivision lot 2 on Union Bluff from Frank L. Sanders for $212. [399/137]

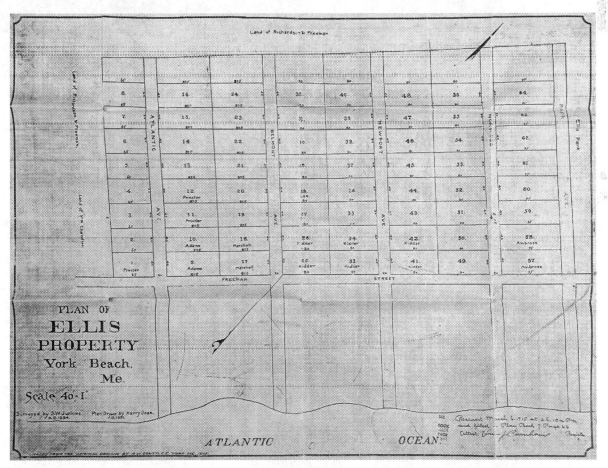

This is a 1915 tracing of Union Bluff land surveyed by Samuel W. Junkins in 1884 for Ellen Ellis and drawn up by Harry Jose in 1891. Lots on this plan were small at only 80 x 40 feet on average, and eight unnumbered lots at the top were described as swampland. Note that Atlantic, Belmont, Newport, and Norwood avenues still exist today, but Park Avenue and the open land on the right called Ellis Park do not. This Ellis Park exists today as Rosewood Lane, a seven-home development. [Plan 7/66] *(York County Registry of Deeds)*

Hazen Ellis's 1884 building is at the upper left with the words "Recreation Hall" written across the roof (Museums of Old York) The July 13, 1977 issue of York County Coast Star *identified four of the girls in this photo as: Josephine Moseley Sanborn Pope, Hattie Garmon Woodeson, Sophie Bowden Smith, and Louise Campbell. Lydia Josephine Moseley, born in 1881, was the daughter of Carlos B. Moseley of Concord, NH, and was three years old in 1884. She married Frank W. Sanborn in 1904, had three children, divorced, and married Kenneth B. Pope in 1936. (Ancestry.com) Sophie V. Bowden, born in 1874, was ten years old in 1884. On October 1, 1904 she married Frank W. Smith, M.D., just two weeks after he had cofounded York Hospital along with six other doctors. They had two children. (January 25, 2006 issue of the* York Weekly, Unknown History of York *by Peter A. Moore)*

1884

- *June 7,* Ellen Ellis purchased pasture land at Union Bluff from Edward Norton for $150. [400/304]

- *June 12,* Hazen Ellis transferred subdivision lots 13 through 18 purchased from Nathaniel Shattuck on September 18, 1883 to Ellen Ellis. [396/383]

Roller Skating Rink

June 4, Ellen Ellis purchased a 4-acre parcel of tillage and waste land from Charles E. Bowden for $800. This was bounded by land of Henry Bowden, land of Josiah Norton, Ocean Ave. [400/303]

June 5, Ellen Ellis purchased land from Josiah Norton for $25, bounded by a willow tree, sand bank, old county road, and land of Charles E. Bowden. [400/305]

These two parcels of empty land evolved into the Ocean House property.

The invention of quad roller skates in 1863, a wheel and axle assembly and toe stop in 1876, and finally the pin ball bearing in 1884 sparked the first of several roller sport boom periods. (Reference: About.com, Sports, quad-skate-history.htm)

There is no evidence in the deeds that there was a pre-existing building on the Short Sands Beach properties purchased by Ellen Ellis in 1884 or that anyone other than Hazen Ellis had constructed the building seen in this photograph. There is a later reference to Recreation Hall in the description of adjacent property Ellen Ellis purchased from Josiah Norton on September 10, 1886. [411/394]

Although the railroad and electric trolleys had not arrived in York Beach yet, there were several boarding houses operating near Short Sands Beach by 1884 that could provide patrons for Recreation Hall (*Annual Register of Maine*, Museums of Old York):

- Concordville:
  - ☐ Bay View House operated by J.B. Brown
  - ☐ Concord House operated by Ruben B. Morgan
- Union Bluff:
  - ☐ Agamenticus House operated by M. S. Griffin
  - ☐ Fairmount House operated by G. S. Varney
  - ☐ Union Bluff House operated by Moses French
  - ☐ Thompson House operated by Henry E. Evans

1885

The Report of the Receipts and Expenditures of the Town of York, Me., year ending February 1886, indicates that sometime between March 1885 and February 1886 Hazen Ellis paid $5 for and received a permit to operate a roller skating rink.

The same publication indicates that the town paid Hazen Ellis for improvements he made in 1885 to the road passing in front of his building: "H. Z. Ellis, allowance for labor on and material for the road from Concordville to Union Bluff, across Short Sands Beach, $55.17."

1886

Ellen Ellis continued to buy Short Sands Beach land this year and the next:

- *September 10,* Ellen Ellis purchased two parcels of ocean front land from Josiah Norton for $50. The first was bounded by land of Ellen Ellis, corner of Recreation Hall, land of Josiah Norton, and the Atlantic Ocean. The second was located southeast of the above parcel and adjacent to land purchased by Ellen Ellis the same day from Charles E. Bowden. [411/394]
- This same day Ellen Ellis purchased a parcel of mowing and waste land from Charles E. Bowden for $1. Bounded by the corner of former Walter Bowden's land to former Joel Norton's land to Atlantic Ocean on Short Sands to Ocean Avenue. [411/395]
- *September 24,* Ellen Ellis purchased land from Abbie P. Norton for $400. Northeast of Short Sands Brook, bounded by Ocean Avenue, bridge over brook, land of Josiah Norton, Old County Road. [414/26]

1887

The town's annual *Report of the Receipts and Expenditures* noted that Hazen Ellis was paid for more improvements he made to the road passing in front of his building during the previous year: "H. Z. Ellis, money expended as per appropriation of town for road across Short Sands in full, $100"

- *January 5,* Ellen Ellis purchased land near Cape Neck from Josiah Norton for $1. This parcel was bounded northeasterly by the Atlantic Ocean, easterly by land which Ellen Ellis had previously purchased from Charles E. Bowden, southerly and southwesterly by the old road leading over Cape Neck (Ocean Avenue Extension), and northwesterly by Short Sands Brook. [411/552] The above five purchases formed the basis of Short Sands Park later this same year.

- *January 5,* Ellen Ellis purchased additional land from Josiah Norton for $1000. This land was bounded northwesterly by the road leading from Josiah Norton's house to Union Bluff (Railroad Avenue), lot started at the corner of Norton house lot, road from that house to Union Bluff, corner of Steven Adams house lot, wall of Armenius H. Bowden land, Short Sands Brook, road leading over Cape Neck so-called, house lot of William Howe. [414/279] This purchase includes a portion of downtown York Beach.

The Goldenrod

June 10, Hazen Ellis built a three story structure with gambrel roof and gable on land purchased from the Norton family on January 5, and in June, he and Ellen Ellis sold this land and building for $2,000 to 57-year old Samuel Ramsdell. [414/438] Samuel was a baker from Dover, NH, and operated it as Ramsdell's Café. Nine years later, in 1896, Edward Talpey took over management of the business and later his wife Martha purchased the property and renamed it the Goldenrod. Edward produced candy by day and ice cream in the evening, later adopting a recipe for taffy that was hand wrapped by employees until machinery was purchased around 1925. (From a presentation narrated by Cheryl Farley of the Old York Historical Society, produced by Aroundmaine. com, and programmed for the web by Chad Farley, March 13, 2006.) The Goldenrod continues operation today with Talpey and Boston descendants producing about 8 million pieces of taffy each year.

Railroad Service

August 8, The York Harbor & Beach Railroad started scheduled service to York, synchronized with the Boston to Portsmouth train every day during daylight hours. At first the route ended at Long Sands Station, which was temporarily named York Beach Station, but once the track was laid through a mile and a half of difficult swamp a few months later the service was extended to Union Bluff. Long Sands Station then became a stop on the route to York Beach Station. At first locomotives were attached at the front and

Ocean House at left c. 1887; the Goldenrod, a.k.a. Ramsdell's Café, is to the right of the gazebo; and the building to the left of the gazebo with two flags was a Casino. (Museums of Old York)

York Beach Station c. 1890. (Author's collection)

Hazen Ellis was no doubt one of the business people who encouraged the Boston and Maine Railroad to build a connection from Portsmouth to York Beach. The railroad had previously bypassed York and made possible the rapid development of beach communities such as Old Orchard Beach further north. Starting around 1885, Hazen adapted his Recreation Hall to get ready for an expected boom in the hotel business. He raised the Recreation Hall hip roof by one level, setting up a dining room, lobby, and lounges in the former hall and sleeping rooms on the second floor with an open space in the middle. On the southwest corner of the dining room he built a kitchen wing and on the north end of the original building he added three floors of sleeping quarters with a porch surrounding the first floor.

rear of the train but later a turntable was built in front of the engine house beyond the York Beach Station and only one engine was required.

The back of Ocean House c. 1887 from the railroad station platform (Museums of Old York)
From left to right: Rockaway Hotel, Frank Ellis cottage, Old Annex, and Ocean House. The windmill can be seen above the dining room, the Old Annex was later moved out back and used as a girl's dorm, a small gazebo was located near the boardwalk running from the train station to Ocean House, and there is an entrance arch over the boardwalk on the far right that says "Ocean House."

Short Sands Park

August 15, Ellen N. Ellis along with Carlos B. Moseley and William G. Gannon conveyed what is now called Ellis Short Sands Park to Carlos B. Moseley, William G. Gannon, Hazen Z. Ellis, Charles L. Bowden, James A. Edgeley, and Channey W. Clement, as trustees, for $1. This land was located between Concordville and Union Bluff and bounded by Short Sands Brook along the road in front of Ocean House, to Concordville to Long Sands road, Concordville road to the bridge on said road, along a row of trees set out by Ellen Ellis to the ocean, to a brook running between Ocean House and Union Bluff, to the point of beginning.

"The land herein conveyed is to be forever used and occupied by the public for a Park and is not to be enclosed by a fence or wall of any description and is to be forever under the management and control of the Trustees, their successors and assigns.

"The Trustees shall have power to organize and select from their number a President, Secretary and Treasurer and adopt suitable By Laws for the protection and management and improvement of said Park. The unanimous consent of the Trustees shall be required to increase their number and in case of the death of a Trustee or the refusal of any one to act for one year the remaining Trustees by unanimous consent may appoint another in his place, but in all other matters a majority shall have power to act. No building not of a public nature shall be erected on said Park, but all buildings and plank walks shall be allowed to remain so long as they shall be kept by the owners in good repair to the satisfaction of the trustees." [418/34]

1888

From the *Report of the Receipts and Expenditures of the Town of York, Me. 1888,* under Miscellaneous Bills 1887 and 1888: "H. Z. Ellis, rebuilding bridge and filling in near the same at Union Bluff, $25.00"

June 29, Ellen Ellis purchased land near Union Bluff from Arthur H. Noyes for $400. This land was located on the easterly side of the road leading from the railroad station to Cape Neddick Village, bounded on the southwesterly side of the new road leading from the Cape Neddick road to the Concordville road, and Bay Street. [419/401] This is another portion of downtown York Beach today.

George H. Walker map, 1888 (Museums of Old York) Legend:
J *Ocean House* **Y** *Hotel Rockaway* **K** *the Atlantic* **L** *Fairmount House*
M *Agamenticus House* **N** *Union Bluff House* **Q** *Ocean House stables*
S *Pierce's Grocery* **V** *railroad station* **R** *post office*

Romie Mae Ellis (Museums of Old York)

November 24, Romie Mae Ellis married postmaster Charles Lord Bowden, brother of Armenius H. Bowden and a cousin of Charles E. Bowden.

1889

March 29, Excerpt from the local news section of the *Biddeford Journal*: "Messrs. Ellis & sons, proprietors of the Ocean House, are to tear down their old stable and build a larger one on its site."

May 3, Excerpt from the local news section of the *Biddeford Journal*: "H.Z. Ellis offers to give a five hundred dollar lot on his new street to anyone that will put up a fine cottage. This is for the purpose of starting the new street with a fine class of houses. The site is located near the Ocean House with a fine ocean view."

October 25, Frank Hazen Ellis married Marietta McDuffee of Dover, NH. She had come to York Beach to visit friends whose father ran Pierce's Grocery Store across the street from the Ocean House stables when she met Frank and fell in love. (May 24, 2000 issue of the *York Weekly,* Unknown History of York by Peter A. Moore)

October 30, Frank Ellis purchased a 75 x 125 foot parcel of land from Hazen and Ellen Ellis for $1 and other valuable consideration. This land was located on the southeasterly side of Frank Street (now Hawk Street) and the southwesterly side of the new road from Union Bluff to Concordville (now Ocean Avenue). [442/38] Frank and Marietta constructed a two-story cottage on this lot which was located in between the Ocean House and Rockaway hotels. The cottage, known for over a century as the Cavanaugh Cottage, still exists today with its distinctive keyhole shaped entry to the front porch.

1890

June 16, Ellen Ellis consolidated title to land on Pleasant and Bay Streets for $335 using Arthur H. Noyes as an intermediary. [441/56]

October 4, Frank Ellis purchased land from Ellen and Hazen Ellis for $1 and other valuable consideration. This land was bounded by the road from the railroad station to Union Bluff, land of Arthur E. Noyes, Bay Street, and land of Andrew J. Kidder. This included the Ocean House stables and all other buildings thereon. [442/39]

1891

April 16, Ellen Ellis conveyed an undivided one-fourth part of her properties in York to Fannie Ellis for $1 and other valuable consideration, [443/101] and another undivided

The Ellis family in front of Seaford Cottage and Ocean House, 1889. (Museums of Old York)
From left to right: unidentified fish vendor, Frank Ellis, Marietta Ellis, Mina Emery, Willard J. Simpson, Fred Ellis, and Fannie Ellis. Frank Ellis and Marietta (McDuffee) were married this year; Willard Simpson and Fannie Ellis married in 1892; Fred Ellis and Mina Emery married in 1896. The willow trees at the curve in Ocean Avenue are on the left, the Seaford Cottage is on the hill, and the stairs leading to the Ocean House kitchen are on the right.

The Comet, Ocean House, Ocean House stables, Frank Ellis's cottage c. 1890. (Author's collection)

The Comet c. 1890. (Museums of Old York)
The Comet was operated from 1889 to 1892 by John C. Staples. It rolled down the tracks into the ocean and was pulled back up by a steam powered winch seen in the shelter on the left. The people are standing on a U-shaped metal structure and a dory in the center would float inside the structure.

one-fourth part to Fred Ellis for similar consideration. [443/102] The properties were:

- From Nathaniel H. Shattuck on September 18, 1883, lots 13 through 18 on Union Bluff [392/532]

- From Charles E. Bowden on June 4, 1884, four acres [400/303]

- From Josiah Norton on June 5, 1884 [400/305]

- From Edward H. Norton on June 7, 1884 [400/304]

- From Josiah Norton on September 10, 1886 [411/394]

- Two parcels from Josiah Norton on January 5, 1887 [411/522, 414/279]

September 5, Hazen Ellis purchased five lots in Concordville from George A. Lord for $340: [446/477]

- Lots 22 and 23 on Broadway Street next to land of C. B. Moseley in Section 1. [Plan 4/13]

- Lot 71 adjoining Broadway Street and Rockland Avenue and lots 72 and 73 adjoining and between Rockland Avenue and a division line, all in Section 3. [Plan 4/15]

1892

June 24, Fannie Ellis, age 23, married Willard J. Simpson, age 28, of York, Maine. Willard was later employed in the management and operation of both the Ocean House and Harmon Hall (until his death on April 27, 1932), and his brother Joseph W. Simpson was treasurer of both the Marshall House and the Emerson.

November 14, Fred Ellis purchased three lots of land from Josiah Chase for $350. These were designated lots 87, 88, and 89 in an Ogunquit Village subdivision next to the Marginal Way. [455/89]

Town meeting Warrant Article 22 in *The Report of the Receipts and Expenditures of the Town of York, Me.,* Year Ending February 1893: "To see if the town will instruct the Selectmen to appoint two or more Fire Wards at York Beach, by request of Frank H. Ellis and ten others." (Museums of Old York)

Fannie Ellis in a promotional photo for the Ellis Family Bell Ringers c. 1885. (Museums of Old York)

1893

February 25, Fred Ellis purchased one lot of land from Josiah Chase for $410. This was designated as lot 78 in an Ogunquit Village subdivision next to the Marginal Way. [455/90]

The same day Fred purchased Concordville subdivision lots 71, 72, and 73 from Hazen Ellis for $1. [455/385] These were three of the five lots Hazen purchased from Carlos B. Moseley on September 5, 1891. [Plan 4/15]

July 21, News item in the *York Courant* as republished in *The Origins of Modern York* by S. Thompson Viele, 2004: "F. H. Ellis had a telephone put into his stable last week."

October 9, Frank Ellis conveyed three lots of land to his wife Marietta Ellis for $1 and other consideration. [459/159] These lots were:

- Purchased from Hazen and Ellen on October 30, 1889, and now included their cottage. [442/38]

- Purchased from Hazen and Ellen on October 4, 1890, and included the Ocean House stables. [442/39]

- Purchased from Henry E. Evans on June 2, 1893, a strip adjacent to their lot. [456/183]

October 12, Ellen Ellis took title to land and buildings previously purchased by Fred Ellis, Fannie Simpson and herself for $2. This was a 77 x 105 foot parcel at the intersection of Marietta and Ocean avenues with the house known as Terrace Villa. [444/502] This was the Ellis family residence at the time and is now known as York Manor.

1894

August 14, Ellen and Fred Ellis and Fannie Simpson purchased lot 37 on the east side of Atlantic Avenue from George Lord for $115. [462/375] This duplicate named Atlantic Avenue is now known as Kendall Road, and

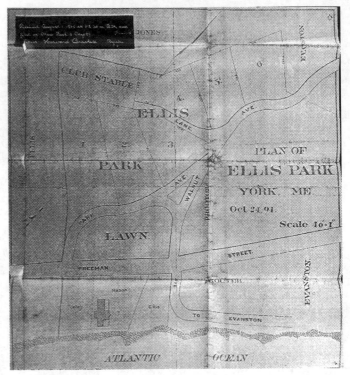

Ellis Park [Plan: 5/89] *(York County Registry of Deeds)*

is located between Ocean Avenue Extension and Broadway Street in Concordville.

August 28, Hazen, Ellen, and Fred Ellis and Fannie Simpson purchased land from Samuel G. Donnell for $314. This property consisted of lots 53 and 54 in a subdivision drawn by Dennett and Jose [Plan 3/43] on November 2, 1893, with 80 feet of frontage on Long Beach Road and extending back to the York Harbor and Beach Railroad. [463/160]

October 24, A plan for a subdivision on Union Bluff called Ellis Park [Plan 5/89] was drawn by civil engineers Dennett and Jose for the Ellis family. This was adjacent to their 1884 64-lot subdivision and featured six lots, a grassy area, and a club stable. This area, on the northwest side of Freeman Street, is now called Rosewood Lane and occupied by seven condominiums.

1895

June 5, The cornerstone was put in place for the Union Church across from Parson's Store. Armenius H. Bowden, Romie Ellis Bowden's brother-in-law, became prosperous sailing on several coasters and schooners as cook, seaman, mate, master and owner from 1861 to 1874. On October 2, 1882, he bought his father George's farm on what became Church Street near the intersection with Long Beach Avenue. In 1885 he built a cottage, in 1886 a barn, in 1887 a two-story house and in 1893 a post office and store. Part of this land he donated as a site for the Union Church, which was constructed by volunteers in 1895, and is known today as the Union Congregational Church. (*Biographical Review*, 1896, York Public Library)

October 22, Hazen, Ellen, Fred and Fannie Ellis repurchased subdivision lot 13 on Union Bluff from William H. Hogarth for $1 and other valuable consideration. [476/254] William Hogarth had purchased the same lot from Hazen, Ellen, Fred and Fannie on June 26, 1894. [464/44]

1896

May 1, News item in the *York Courant* as republished in *The Origins of Modern York* by S. Thompson Viele, 2004: "Frank Ellis received from Boston last Monday, two handsome sticks of timber—southern pine 12 x 14, 58 feet long, for moving large buildings."

May 20, Fred A. Ellis married Mina Pearl Emery, the daughter of the first York Harbor and Beach Railroad locomotive engineer Thomas B. Emery.

Union Congregational Church. (Author's collection)

September 11, Advertisement in the *York Courant* as republished in *The Origins of Modern York* by S. Thompson Viele, 2004:

"FOR SALE. A Manville wind tower about 60 feet. Tank about 4,000 gallons capacity. Also, a Dean Steam Pump, practically new having been used but two summers. Reason for selling: the introduction of Chase lake water. Also two good cows. F. A. Ellis and Co."

Concordville hotels, operating in 1896, as listed in the *Annual Register of Maine* (Museums of Old York):

The wind tower and tank at Ocean House c. 1890 with "The Comet" amusement ride tracks in the foreground. (Author's collection)

York Beach hotels in Concordville. (Author's collection)

- Bay View House, operated by J. B. Brown was first listed in 1882 and is now a private residence

- Concord House, operated by Ruben B. Morgan was first listed in 1882, and later became the Albatross Hotel. It was destroyed by fire on May 21, 1968

- Katahdin House, operated by Nathaniel H. Shattuck was first listed in 1896, and is now known as the Katahdin Inn and operated by Robert and Rae LeBlanc

- The Worthen, operated by C. L. Worthen was not listed until 1906, and is now a condominium complex known as the Massachusetts

- The Fairview, operated by G. E. Gordon was first listed in 1896, and no longer exists

Trolley Service

1897

June 9, From A History of the York Beach Fire Department 1890–1990 by John D. Bardwell and Peter A. Moore and printed by Peter E. Randall:

"The first mention of the York Beach Hose Company No. 1 was on June 9, 1897 when Hazen Z. Ellis, Ellen N. Ellis, Mina P. Ellis, W. J. Simpson, and Fannie M. Simpson deeded a parcel of land on Bay Street and Pleasant Street to Frank H. Ellis, W. C. Hildreth, and E. A. Talpey, trustees of the York Beach Hose Company No. 1. 'The above lot of land to be used for building and storage of the property belonging to said Fire Company.'"

August 27, The first electric street railway car from Portsmouth arrived in front of the Goldenrod.

York Beach, Me, the Square. (Author's collection)

November 19, News item in the *York Courant* as republished in *The Origins of Modern York* by S. Thompson Viele, 2004:

"A group of citizens met at the house of Fred A. Ellis on Wednesday evening and formed a Citizens' Protective Association for the suppression of the sale of liquor, gambling and kindred evils."

Buildings from left to right: Lessard Cottage, Terrace Villa, Seaford Cottage, Ocean House kitchen and dining room. (Author's collection)

1898

June 7, Hazen, Fred, and Mina Ellis and Fannie Simpson transferred a 30 x 150 foot strip of land to Ellen Ellis for $1 and other consideration. This strip was located in between the Terrace Villa cottage and the Ocean House property. [486/313]

June 10, News item in the *York Courant* as republished in *The Origins of Modern York* by S. Thompson Viele, 2004: "George N. Thompson is doing a very nice job of wiring on the new and elegant bath house of Hartley W. Mason. Mr. Thompson has also just contracted to wire the Ocean House at York Beach for electric lights from the plant of Hon. E. S. Marshall."

June 30, Hazen and Ellen Ellis conveyed the northwest half of the Terrace Villa cottage and lot to Fred Ellis for $1 and other consideration. A dividing line began on Ocean Avenue, ran past the westerly side of the steps leading into the cottage, along the northwesterly side of the lower hall and onward to the rear of the lot. Common areas were defined as: the front steps; the lower and upper hall, the stairs leading to the upper hall; the bathroom; the laundry; the cellar; the parlor on the northwesterly side

of the lower hall; the back stairway; the back bathroom. [492/532]

October 7, An advertisement in the *York Courant* as republished in *The Origins of Modern York* by S. Thompson Viele, 2004: "You can live right in your house, eat drink and sleep without even taking down your chimneys or fireplaces if you let Frank H. Ellis move your buildings."

1899

May 29, Ellen Ellis purchased Fannie Simpson's interest in the Ocean House property for $500. This was bounded by: Ocean Avenue; Marietta Avenue; lands of R. G. Sullivan, Samuel Bowden, Henry Bowden, A. H. Bowden, Stephen Adams, York Harbor and Beach Railroad; Bay Avenue; Pleasant Avenue; Frank Avenue; and by land conveyed to Ellen by Fred Ellis on the same day. This included Fannie's interest in the stable situated on the above described land. [500/146]

September 28, News item in *The Old York Transcript* as republished in *The Origins of Modern York* by S. Thompson Viele, 2004: "F. H. Ellis will shortly begin work on the raising and moving back of the old Emerson mansion at York Village upon which extensive repairs will be made."

October 12, Among the advertisers in this issue of *The Old York Transcript* as republished in *The Origins of Modern York* by S. Thompson Viele, 2004: "Willard J. Simpson Hardware Store, York Harbor" and "F. H. Ellis, practical building mover, York Beach"

October 17, Marietta Ellis purchased lot 20 from the York Cliffs Improvement Company for $1,500. There were stipulations attached with the purchase:

"First: Said lot is to be used for residence purposes only.

"Second: No stable, outhouse, windmill, cesspool or any other structure which may be objectionable to other owners of lots in the vicinity shall be erected or established thereon nor any fences built or erected thereon without the express consent of the York Cliffs Improvement Company by its successors or assigns in writing.

"Third: No house shall be erected on said lot within thirty feet of the outside line of the street.

"Fourth: Said grantee agrees to erect a house upon said lot to cost not less than five thousand dollars and to have the same completed and ready for occupancy on or before the first day of June A.D. 1900 and to place said house on said lot equally distant from the boundary lines between said lot on lots numbered sixteen (16) and twenty-one (21)

"And the York Cliff Improvement Company stipulates and agrees with the said grantee that similar conditions shall be imposed upon all future purchasers of residence lots as are herein imposed upon said grantee."

The same day Marietta Ellis provided an unsecured loan of $6,000 to John D. Vermeule of New York City (president of the York Cliffs Improvement Company) and Joseph N. Kenney of York Cliffs, Maine. This was written up as a mortgage and strangely stipulated that the obligation could be voided at the discretion of the Improvement Company. At face value, this would appear to be the cost of constructing a home, but that is not mentioned. It was mentioned that lot 20 was under attachment, as recorded at the Registry of Deeds, to satisfy a judgment that may be rendered against the Improvement Company. [505/314]

Joseph Kenney's home in the York Cliffs development is one of the few originals still remaining. It is now known as Greystone Manor, can be clearly seen from Short Sands Beach, and is occasionally used as a wedding venue.

The following are all news items in *The Old York Transcript* as republished in *The Origins of Modern York* by S. Thompson Viele, 2004:

- *November 16,* "The foundation and basement of the old Emerson mansion which has been moved back by Frank H. Ellis is complete and the property already shows decided improvement in its appearance. The house was moved so carefully that none of the plastering showed a single crack by the operation."

- "Frank H. Ellis and his crew of men began work on Tuesday morning to raise the Lyman owned by Mr. Hogarth at York Beach. The work will prove difficult but it is just the kind of contract in which Mr. Ellis takes a special pride in performing. The building will be raised twelve feet and a story built underneath, making four stories in all. Its size is forty by fifty feet and contains four chimneys and fireplaces."

- *November 23,* "Willard J. Simpson has decided that he will not build Roaring Rock Inn this year as contemplated. The increased price of building material and construction and the unavailability of certain proposed means of cooperation are among his chief reasons of his change of plans. While the idea is not wholly abandoned, however, he will postpone his efforts in this direction indefinitely and, it is understood, will build one or more handsome cottages near the present hotel site, which is one of the finest locations on the coast. Much of the lumber which was purchased for the building, being unsuitable for other purposes, will be shipped to Boston for re-sale."

- *December 21,* "The final work of mounting the cannon at the Village is being performed by F. H. Ellis."

1900

- *March 1,* "F. H. Ellis has taken the contract to move the old Baptist church at York Corner which is the property of Charles E. Grant, to land near the Christian church. The building will be made over into a dwelling house."

- *April 12,* "Through the agency of H. E. Evans, F. H. Ellis has bought an acetylene gas plant with a capability of 40 lights for his new cottage at York Cliffs."

June 29, Hazen, Ellen, and Fred Ellis sold a 120 x 80 foot parcel of land with buildings thereon to Frank's wife Marietta Ellis for $400. This land was located in the vicinity of the Goldenrod. [524/118]

- *October 4,* "The summer residents of York Beach have contributed toward the building and maintenance of a Catholic church which will be erected before another season on land next to Parson's Grocery Store purchased by A. H. Bowden."

- *October 25,* "W. S. Putnam has given to F. H. Ellis the contract to raise his house ten feet for the purpose of building another story under it."

1901

- *March 21,* "The Catholic church at York Beach will be located in the Diocese of Maine while it will be built and largely attended and supported by people from Manchester and other parts of New Hampshire. Whether it will be under the direct control of the Bishop of Maine or Bishop Bradley of Manchester will not be determined until after a successor of the late Bishop of Portland is appointed and consecrated. This will in no way hold back the building operations, however, which will be proceeded with as early as possible in order to have the chapel ready for occupancy next summer. The name for the chapel, of course, will be a matter for the bishop to decide at that time

Star of the Sea Catholic Church. (Author's collection)

when the oversight of the new house of worship is fixed."

1902

January 29, Hazen and Ellen Ellis transferred the York Beach property which included the Ocean House, the Seaford Cottage, the Old Annex, and the New Annex to Fred Ellis for $1 and other valuable consideration. [517/138]

The same day, Fred and Mina Ellis borrowed $4,000 from Ellen and Hazen Ellis, using the Ocean House properties as collateral. This mortgage was to be paid off within five years at an annual interest rate of 5 percent. [512/454] This mortgage was not paid off for reasons that will become evident in 1904, and eventually became the undoing of Ellis family ownership of Ocean House.

October 17, News item in *The Old York Transcript* as republished in *The Origins of Modern York* by S. Thompson Viele, 2004, "Work on the rebuilding of the Reading Room's clubhouse by contractor Goodwin is advancing rapidly. The building has been turned around and set back several feet from the road. This part of the work was done by F. H. Ellis."

1903

August 24, Ellen McDuffee discharged a mortgage [529/345] granted to her by her daughter Marietta McDuffee Ellis on April 16, 1901. [512/110]

Sometime before October 1904 Fred A. Ellis published a brochure entitled *The Ocean House, York Beach, Maine.* The text and two photographs from that brochure follow below. (U-Maine Orono, Special Collections):

*"And in the deepening shades of night
The Nubble Light gleams o'er the spray,
Boon Island too from far away
At sea shines steadily and bright.*

"An Ideal Summer Resort

"**York Beach** on the coast of Maine is only two hours ride from Boston and seven from New York, where through trains and every convenience of transportation is at the service of the traveler. The Ocean House is situated on a bluff fifty feet above sea-level, directly over the beach and commanding one of the grandest views on the Maine coast. The Hotel and Cottages provide all the comforts and conveniences known to modern life and will accommodate 250 guests.

"**Broad Piazzas** around the entire Hotel overlook the rocky shore, and beach in front, the pretty villas and forests in the rear, and Mount Agamenticus in the distance. Both ocean and country views are unsurpassed. The Hotel grounds present a sea frontage of 1,200 feet.

"**The Hotel's Interior** is comfortable and cheerful throughout. The visitor first enters a broad hall, warmed on cold days by a large fireplace. Adjoining is a homelike parlor and music room, and opposite is the dining hall, the entire length of which overlooks the sea. The sleeping rooms are mostly en suite and are provided with the very best of beds. Every window presents a magnificent view either inland or ocean. The drainage is perfect. The sanitary arrangements are of the most modern and approved methods. A large volume of water flows continually through closets and drains.

"**The Cuisine** of the Ocean House is famous for its excellence. The table is supplied daily with fresh vegetables, rich milk and cream from adjacent farms. Abundance of fish, clams and lobsters are obtained from the local market. The purest of water is supplied from Chase Lake, a large and beautiful body of water nestling among the hills six miles distant. The table will always be maintained at the very highest standard.

"**The Amusements** to be enjoyed in connection with the Ocean House are of greater variety than can be found at any resort on the North Atlantic coast. The country drives are unsurpassed. The roads are maintained in the best condition for Carriage, Automobile and Bicycle. Buckboard rides along shore, through beautiful country ways and forests and to the mountain are ever a source of pleasure.

"**Tennis** The Hotel has tennis and croquet grounds and a fine baseball field. A good orchestra furnishes music for the numerous hops, germans [sic] and social entertainments regularly maintained by the management. And for social prominence alone, the Ocean House is regarded with most popular favor.

"**Surf Bathing** is one of the most healthful and delightful pastimes at this resort, and there is no spot on the coast that offers more attractive facilities than the beautiful hard beach directly in front of the Hotel. Adults and children can bathe with perfect safety. Connected with the Hotel are commodious bath houses with all modern accessories, including shower baths, etc. . . .

"**Trolley Rides** are one of the most enjoyable pastimes for the summer visitor that can be imagined, and prove very popular to all who come to York. The ride along the shore

HOTEL OFFICE

The office, lobby, front entry door, and fireplace in Ocean House, c. 1903. (U-Maine Orono, Special Collections) Note the surface mounted wiring and pear shaped Edison light bulbs installed in June 1898.

DINING HALL

Tables in the dining room, looking east, c. 1903. (U-Maine Orono, Special Collections)

Ocean House, York Beach, Maine. *This is where we are stopping until Sept. 1st. We go in bathing in the surf every day and enjoy every minute. Children are having a gala time. Mabel S. Bates.*

Published in Germany by Ko Tsuboyama & Co. York Beach, Maine.

Trolley passing in front of Ocean House heading for the station located near the Goldenrod. (Phil Meader)

and through the woods to Portsmouth is noted as the most beautiful and picturesque spot in all New England. It brings into easy access nearly every part of the historic old town of York and to ride in the large and comfortable open cars on a midsummer day, beside the sea, is a luxury worth many times the small price of fare. It is now possible to go from York Beach to Boston by trolley, and presently to Portland. . . .

The boardwalk and bridge on Short Sands Beach, Terrace Villa on the far right, c. 1904. (Author's collection)

"**York Beach** is a combination of sea-coast, mountains and country. Its shores are rugged and grand, indented by beautiful sandy beaches. York Beach is conspicuous for its unsurpassed surf bathing, its absence of mosquitoes, its rural environments, its perfect sewerage system, its refined and select patronage with an absence of the rough element often found at seaside resorts. On the hottest days an ocean breeze will temper the atmosphere to a coolness most refreshing and invigorating."

Three Years of Tragedy

October 11, Fred Hazen Ellis, the 11 year old son of son of Frank H. and Marietta Ellis, passed away. Another son, born to Frank and Marietta five years later in 1908, was given the same name.

1904

October 22, Fred A. Ellis the owner-operator of the Ocean House hotel, resident of York Village, and twin brother of Frank H. Ellis died at age 44. He was survived by his wife Mina (they had no children).

December 24, Ellen, Mina, Hazen, Frank, and Fannie Ellis granted to Romie Bowden entitlement to a one-sixth interest in proceeds from the sale of any lands now held by Ellen N. Ellis and Mina P. Ellis east of Marietta Avenue, and also land held by Ellen, Mina, Frank, and Fannie Ellis at Union Bluff. [574/213]

1905

October 25, Mina P. Ellis, the widow of Fred A. Ellis, died at age 30, one year after Fred.

October 28, Three days after Mina's death, Ellen N. Ellis died at age 74.

No documentation was found to explain four untimely deaths in the Ellis family, but there was a typhoid fever epidemic in progress in eastern Maine during the same years. In 1903, Waterville, Augusta, and other towns downstream using the Kennebec River as a source for the public water supply were ravaged, and in 1904, Millinocket, Bangor, Old Town, Brewer, and downstream towns on the Penobscot River were severely affected. Attitudes toward dumping of sewerage into rivers and inadequate water filtration started to change that year. (Reference: the April 19, 2004 edition of the *Bangor Daily News*) With the hotel season finished by September, one has to wonder if there was a late September or early October annual event in one of the affected towns that attracted the Ellis family and exposed them to the sometimes fatal disease.

December 5, In the Will of Ellen Ellis, she first gave all of her estate for the use of Hazen. Fourthly she gave the residue of her estate equally to Romie Bowden, Fannie Simpson, Fred and Frank Ellis. After Fred died, she had modified the will to give the use of her cottage Terrace Villa to Fred's widow Mina and after her death to Romie, Fannie, and Frank. [532/375]

The Will of Mina Ellis was probated on the same day. She gave the use of her half of the cottage Terrace Villa to Hazen and Ellen who lived in the other half of the cottage, and the remainder of her property to her legal heirs according to the laws governing distribution of intestate estates. Her father, railroad locomotive engineer Thomas B. Emery, was named executor. [532/376]

1908

March 26, Frank Ellis purchased the 1902 Ocean House mortgage [512/454] from Romie Bowden, Fannie Simpson, and Hazen Ellis, as the heirs of Ellen Ellis, for $4,000. [574/210] Frank was now the legal owner of Ocean House.

The same day the heirs transferred land from Ellen's estate to Frank Ellis for $1 and other valuable consideration. [574/211] Referenced deeds were: [395/340, 400/303, 411/552, 444/502, and 486/313]

Willard J. Simpson, Frank Ellis's brother-in-law and York Harbor businessman, had been managing the Ocean House since Fred Ellis died in 1904. At the beginning of Frank's ownership, 33 year-old Gilman L. Moulton partnered with Willard in the management of Ocean House, and the team of "Simpson & Moulton" was listed in the *Annual Register of Maine* until 1913. In 1917 Gilman became the general manager of the Marshall House hotel complex in York Harbor and Stage Neck, with Willard's younger brother Joseph W. Simpson as his treasurer. Willard stayed on as manager of Ocean House until his death in 1932.

Frank Ellis moved or enlarged many high profile structures in the York area, usually for other people. In 1908 and 1909, he purchased the dance hall at St. Aspinquid Park, then ten years old, and moved it across Main Street and down Hildreth Hill through fields to a site on the left side of Dr. Hawkes Pharmacy. He acquired an opulent colonnaded building façade from Revere Beach and set it up as the Main Street entrance to his complex called the Gay White Way. Inside there was an arcade and lunch room as well as the dance hall, and he built a theater extending out in back of the pharmacy. (Reference: John D. Bardwell's *Images of America Old York Beach*, published by Arcadia Publishing) The pharmacy building still exists but the former Gay White Way complex burned to the ground on March 21, 1951.

1910

April 4, The Saco and Biddeford Savings Institution purchased the 1908 Ocean House mortgage [574/210] from Frank Ellis for $4,000.

Again, the entire Ocean House property was used as security. [590/200]

1916

York Beach Fire Association

May 1, From *A History of the York Beach Fire Department 1890–1990,* by John D. Bardwell and Peter A. Moore, printed by Peter E. Randall:

". . . The York Beach Fire Association was organized as a corporation on May 1, 1916 in the home of Frank Ellis, and registered on June 16, with the Secretary of State in Augusta. The first meeting of the corporation was held on August 1, 1916, and the first board of directors included Charles L. Worthen, President; Frank H. Ellis, Vice President; Harley G. Ellis, Secretary; H. Grant Duff, Treasurer; John D. Keene and George A. Chase. They voted to sell a thousand shares of stock for five dollars per share to purchase land and build a new fire station. Then they

GAY WHITE WAY AND SQUARE, YORK BEACH, ME.

The Gay White Way grand entrance and Dr. Hawkes Pharmacy at center c. 1910 (Author's collection) Signs at left promise that you could have your palm read by Madam Wanita in the "Scientific Palmistry Parlor," have first class photos finished quickly, or have your picture on a postal card that could be mailed.

This is the family of Frank and Marietta Ellis c.1914. Standing, from left to right; Romie, James, Carroll, Harley, Marietta, Mina, and Lawrence; Sitting, from left to right: Fred, Hazel, Fannie, and Frank. Their home in this image, known as the Willows, still exists today at the corner of Long Beach Avenue and Broadway Extension. (Museums of Old York; photo identification from the May 24, 2000 York Weekly Unknown History of York)

began to develop plans for the new building which would also house a Kelly Springfield combination booster and pumper that had been approved at town meeting on March 13, 1916.

"Their planning took on a sense of urgency when the old fire station was destroyed during the Arcade fire [former site of the Ocean House stables]. They sold their original lot to Thomas B. Emery on November 8, 1916. Land for a new fire station was donated by the York Harbor and Beach Railroad, a branch of the Boston and Maine Railroad, on January 2, 1917. 'Said premises are conveyed on the express condition that they be used only

for a fire station, that any building erected thereon shall be of a type acceptable to the grantor, and that upon ceasing to be used as aforesaid, the title of the same shall revert to the grantor, its successors or assigns.'"

1917

July 30, Ownership of Short Sands Park was transferred to the York Beach Village Corporation:

"The land herein conveyed is to be used and occupied forever, by the public for a Park, and is not to be enclosed by a fence or wall of any description and is to be under the management and control of said York Beach Village Corporation its successors and assigns.

"The Corporation shall have power to organize and select a President, Secretary and Treasurer or Trustees, and adopt suitable By-laws for the protection, management and improvement of said 'Park', the unanimous consent of the Officers or Trustees shall be required to increase their number and in case of the death of a Trustee, or the refusal of any one to act for one year, the remaining Trustees by unanimous consent may appoint another in his place, but in all other matters a majority shall have power to act. No building not of a public nature shall be erected on said Park but all buildings and plank walks shall be allowed to remain so long as they shall be kept by the owners in good repair to the satisfaction of the Corporation." 683/397

1918

From the 1918 Ocean House brochure (Author's collection):

"YORK BEACH, the gateway to the State of Maine, is one of the most beautiful summer resorts in New England. Here, only two hours' ride from Boston and eight from New York, are the rugged shores and cool green woods of the Pine Tree State. Hard sand beaches, bays, harbors, rivers and lakes, lend their charm to this delightful spot. Its country is famous for beautiful drives by river banks and lakes, through forests, over hills and mountains. On the hottest days an ocean breeze will temper the atmosphere to coolness most refreshing and invigorating. Thousands of people spend their summers at York Beach, and thousands more find it a convenient and delightful resting place on their way into Maine. YORK BEACH is on the Boston & Maine Railroad, seventy miles from Boston, with through trains and every

FINE PIAZZA LOOKOUT TO THE OCEAN.

convenience of transportation from Boston, New York, Portland and Montreal. It possesses every quality to render it an ideal spot for health, rest and recreation.

"THE OCEAN HOUSE

"In point of location and accessibility, as well as beauty of surroundings, the Ocean House presents every desirable advantage. It is the largest and most modern hotel on the State Road between Portsmouth and Portland. There are broad piazzas around the entire hotel which overlook the beach and ocean in front, attractive farms, forests and hills in the rear, and Mount Agamenticus in the distance, seven miles away. The hotel grounds present a sea frontage of twelve hundred feet and are made attractive by flowers and shrubs.

"THE THREE COTTAGES connected with hotel are especially liked by families and those wishing quiet, homelike surroundings. They are only a few feet from either end of hotel, all rooms having electric lights, and bells connecting with hotel office, and receive the same service as those in the main house.

"TERRACE VILLA has fourteen fine rooms with several private baths and fireplaces.

VIEW OF OCEAN HOUSE AND COTTAGES.

The Annex has sixteen rooms and the smaller cottage has five rooms . . .

"RECREATION

"SUMMER SPORTS afforded in connection with the Ocean House are of great variety. The Hotel has splendid new tennis court and croquet grounds. The York Country Club is devoted to tennis, golf, and social enjoyment. Its membership includes some of the most prominent men in the country, and its luncheons and teas are most delightful affairs. One hundred thousand dollars have been expended in club houses and grounds, and the eighteen-hole golf links are among the finest in America.

"DEEP SEA SAILING and fishing excursions to other shore resorts furnish delightful pastime. Off shore, fishing is good. The canoeing on York River is excellent. Yachts, power boats and canoes are always available.

"SURF BATHING is one of the most healthful and enjoyable pastimes at this resort. Directly in front of the hotel there is a fine hard beach where adults and children can bathe with perfect safety. Connected with the hotel are new bath houses, with modern accessories. The invigorating results of sea bathing at York Beach prove valuable to many health seekers.

"RIDING—Good and safe saddle horses may be hired by the hour, with or without instructors.

"TROLLEY RIDING is a popular pastime. The rides along the shore to Portsmouth and through Eliot and Green Acre on the Piscataqua, and to Wells, Kennebunk and Portland, are noted as the most beautiful and picturesque in New England. They bring into easy access historic parts of York, the Country Club and Golf Links, Kittery and its Navy Yard, Portsmouth, Hampton, Rye Beach and Dover.

"MOTORING

"YORK is now equipped with splendid roads for motoring. The State Highway, a new

OCEAN HOUSE AND BEACH, YORK BEACH, ME.

Short Sands Beach with the Ocean House bath house on the left near the boardwalk, c. 1920. (Author's collection)

The Willows, York Beach, Maine.

Trolley rounding the bend by the Willows before travelling through Short Sands Park, c. 1910. (Author's collection)

and provided with the very best of beds. Hot and cold water and private baths have been installed in a large number of rooms. Every window presents magnificent inland or ocean views. The plumbing and sanitary conditions are of the most modern and approved methods.

"THE CUISINE of the Ocean House is famous for its excellence. The table is supplied daily with fresh vegetables, rich milk, cream and butter from adjacent farms. An abundance of fish, clams and lobsters are obtained from the local market where freshness is absolutely assured. It is the particular aim of the management to maintain the table at the very highest standard.

"The Ocean House garage is new and fire proof.

macadam road, from Portsmouth to Portland, passes directly in front of the Ocean House. The town maintains 150 miles of highway and the country drives are unsurpassed for their beauty. Automobile rides along shore through beautiful country ways and forests, and to Mount Agamenticus with its view for a hundred miles around, are always a source of much pleasure. One may drive every day in the season, and always find new paths, new surprises and new delights.

"COMFORTABLE AND HOMELIKE

"THE INTERIOR of the Ocean House is comfortable and homelike throughout. The visitor first enters a broad lobby, warmed on chilly days by cheerful fires in the large fireplaces. Adjoining this is a parlor and cozy music room. On the other side is the beautiful dining hall, its entire length overlooking the sea. The sleeping rooms are mostly en suite

HOTEL LOBBY.

A CORNER OF THE DINING HALL

1920

December 14, Hazen Z. Ellis, truly a pioneer of York Beach, Maine, died at the age of 96.

1923

March 17, Trolley service to York Beach was discontinued. By now the automobile had become the preferred mode of transportation and, as scenic and nostalgic as it was, the electric street railway passenger fares could no longer cover its expenses.

"A SPECIAL FEATURE is made of providing abundant social amusement for guests, including afternoon teas, concerts, card parties and dances. The hotel orchestra gives daily concerts and provides music for the dancing.

"Ocean House opens for guests on or about June 25th each season. Rates and any further information will be promptly furnished.

"W. J. SIMPSON,
York Beach, Maine."

Both Frank Ellis, with the rank of Captain, and later his son Harley, with rank of Chief Engineer (see photo at right), were commanding officers in the York Beach Fire Department. When the department reorganized in 1929, Harley became Chief of the fire department, serving from 1929 to 1947. (*A History of the York Beach Fire Department 1890–1990* by John D. Bardwell and Peter A. Moore)

Harley's son, Richmond, served in the U.S. Navy aboard the submarine USS Scorpion during World War II and was lost at sea on February 1, 1944, in the South China Sea. (Ancestry.com)

Four generations of the Ellis family in 1918, clockwise from left, Hazen Z., Frank H., Harley G., Richmond H. Ellis. (Museums of Old York)

PARKING SPACE AND BEACH, YORK BEACH, MAINE.
WAHNITA

The increasing popularity of automobiles put an end to trolley and train service to York Beach by 1925. (Author's Collection)

1925

June 29, The York Harbor and Beach Railroad was abandoned except for a spur track servicing the Portsmouth Navy Yard.

1929

January 29, Romie Mae Ellis Bowden died at age 64. Her husband, Charles L. Bowden, had predeceased her on July 31, 1924.

1932

April 27, Willard J. Simpson, the husband of Fannie Ellis Simpson and proprietor of Ocean House, died at age 67. He was survived by his wife Fannie and a daughter Dorothy M. Simpson.

October 10, The Saco and Biddeford Savings Institution, which held a $4,000 mortgage originated in 1902 on the entire Ocean House property, foreclosed on 72 year old Frank Ellis. [834/246] Frank became the owner of Ocean House in 1908 due to the deaths of his twin brother Fred and mother Ellen and relied on Willard Simpson to manage the business. Apparently there were no Ellis heirs interested in taking on the responsibility, and with the country still in the Great Depression, Frank let it go to the bank.

Epilogue

March 30, 1936, Frank H. Ellis died at age 76.

April 20, 1937, His wife Marietta died the next year at age 65. They were survived by four daughters, Hazel E. Hancock, Romie G. Boardman, Mina P. Chase, and Fannie N. Bridges, all of York Beach; four sons, Harley G., Lawrence R., and Carroll C. of York Beach and Fred H. of Akron, Ohio. At the time of Marietta's death, there were 22 grandchildren. (Reference: the May 24, 2000 issue of the *York Weekly,* "Unknown History of York" by Peter A. Moore)

June 29, 1953, Gilman L. Moulton died at age 77. He had a very successful career in hotel management, starting with the Albracca Hotel in York Harbor, [Ocean House in York Beach], the Sparhawk Hotel in Ogunquit, and for 33 years as general manager of the Marshall House hotel complex. Gilman L. Moulton Park, adjacent to former Marshall House land on York Street in York Harbor, was named in his honor for 55 years of dedicated service to his community. (Reference: Historic Marker placed in 1999)

February 20, 1957, Fannie Ellis Simpson died at age 88, survived by her daughter Dorothy M. Simpson.

Camp Family/Ocean House, Inc. Ownership

The Early Years

1910–1931

In 1910 Paul Benjamin Camp, age 24, and Elizabeth Fell Camp, age 21 and known as Bessie, lived with Paul's parents Frank and Annie Camp in Jonesboro, Georgia soon after they were married. By 1920 they had their own house in Jonesboro and two young sons. Robert Fell Camp was born on July 30, 1914, and Franklin Ellis Camp was born on July 16, 1917. Franklin was known within the family by his middle name, Ellis. By 1926 Paul and Bessie had another son, Paul Benjamin Camp Jr. who was born on November 16, 1922, and had moved to Harrison Avenue in Clearwater, Florida. This was near the hotel district and intracoastal waterway, and Paul Sr. took a position as manager of the Clearwater Beach Hotel. In 1931 he left Clearwater and leased the Gulfport Inn (originally the Hotel Dobler) in Gulfport, Florida, southwest of Tampa.

The Boca Ciega Inn

Here is a brief history of the hotel written by Allean Davis in 1984 (Gulfport Historical Society):

"In the beginning it was called the Hotel Dobler, built in 1922 on the corner of 31st Avenue South and 54th Street. It was meant to be an exclusive fishing lodge, but it never really succeeded well. It was a large frame building covered with stucco. The lower floor consisted of a large entrance hall, main lobby, sun porch, dining room, kitchen and pantries. There were 42 rental rooms upstairs, and it also contained an elevator shaft, but no elevator was

The one-year-old Hotel Dobler is in the background in 1923. The Florida Nook Tea Room and the Shell Hunter Shop are in the foreground of the above photo on Shore Boulevard South. These were located on the same spot where On the Rocks and O'Maddy's Bar and Grille are today, across the street from the town beach. This was the third year of Prohibition, and it is suspected that the Tea Room served more than just tea. (Betsy Camp)

ever installed. John Dobler seemed unable to enlarge the hotel, or even manage it very well as only a few guests came and went. He was pistol whipped by local residents because he let his black employees stay in his stable attic after dark. A curfew was in effect in Gulfport at that time, and no black person was allowed to stay in Gulfport from 'sundown to sun-up.' Mr. Dobler never seemed to regain his strength after the attack to complete his plans for the hotel; his spirit seemed completely broken.

The Gulfport Inn, formerly Hotel Dobler, leased by the Camps in 1931. (Betsy Camp)

"Ten years later, in 1932, Mr. and Mrs. Paul B. Camp [Sr.] bought the Hotel Dobler and changed the name to Boca Ciega Inn. The cost was $32,500 for the building and four lots. They also paid $2,500 for furnishings for 42 rental rooms and for dining room and kitchen equipment. A full basement was made into game rooms and a business office was added. Besides the main building there were 4 apartments and 2 cottages facing 31st Avenue South which were rented by season or month. People renting these places also enjoyed the activities of the regular guests, and most of them took their meals at the Inn. It was operated on the American plan with three complete meals a day. Usually there were two hundred people for Sunday dinner, and soon 95% of the guests were booking for the coming year. The guests who returned season after season said it was just like one big happy family getting together again.

Paul B. Sr., Bessie, Robert, and F. Ellis Camp in front of Boca Ciega Inn in November 1937. (Betsy Camp)

"Mr. and Mrs. Camp worked tirelessly as host and hostess, striving to please and make their guests as comfortable as possible. They were competent and careful managers . . . admired and loved by everyone they came

The Boca Ciega Inn, early 1930s. (Betsy Camp) The municipal fishing pier on the left at the end of 54th Street, the fishing party boat "Tarpon" is awaiting clients, and people are swimming in the shallow waters in front of the Inn.

in contact with, and the Inn became successful because two friendly, caring people were in charge of it."

From the Camp's Ocean House/Boca Ciega Inn flyer:

"Boca Ciega Inn, our Florida location, is on the beach at Boca Ciega Bay, which is part of the Gulf of Mexico, and in the City of St. Petersburg. All rooms are provided with hot and cold running water, steam heat, bath rooms, and spacious clothes closets. Three summer houses on the lawn provide delightful places for our guests to sit and watch the boats and other water activities.

"Bathing in the temperate waters of the Gulf is a pleasure that can be enjoyed every day of the year. Our private bathing beach and sulphur pool is on the Inn property. Our beach is safe for children and those who are timid.

"Fishing in Boca Ciega Bay and the Gulf is the fisherman's paradise. The fighting tarpon and kings, also mackerel and other small fish can he caught by the amateur as well as the seasoned fisherman.

"The Inn property adjoins the Gulfport Municipal Pier where deep sea fishing boats leave every day for the Gulf fishing banks (charges from $1.00 to $2.00 per day, including tackle and bait); also where small boats can be rented for private parties or by individuals. Fishing can be enjoyed also from the pier, where many large catches are taken during the season. No charge is made for pier fishing.

"St. Petersburg has been termed the Sunshine City, and is the center of winter activities on the west coast (of Florida), with unsurpassed facilities for bathing, golf, fishing and

Boca Ciega Inn c. 1950. (Betsy Camp)

excursions to Bird and Shell islands, Pass-a-Grille, and other points of tropical and scenic interest. Hourly trips across the bay to the islands for the small charge of 25 cents round trip, where many interesting varieties of sea shells may be collected."

Ocean House

1932

Following the April 27 death of Ocean House manager Willard Simpson, owner Frank Ellis leased the Ocean House to Paul Sr. and Bessie Camp who moved their 1931–1932 winter staff from the Boca Ciega Inn to York Beach for the 1932 summer season.

October 10, the Saco and Biddeford Savings Institution foreclosed on Frank Ellis, taking control of the entire Ocean House property which included Ocean House, Seaford Cottage, Old Annex, and New Annex. [834/246]

1933

"In 1933 Paul B. and Bessie Fell Camp leased the Ocean House property from the Saco and Biddeford Savings Institution . . ." (Superior Court Civil Action Docket No. 9456, December 4, 1968—Bathhouse dispute)

1934

April 12, Paul B. Sr. and Bessie Camp officially purchased the Ocean House property from the Saco and Biddeford Savings Institution for $1 and other valuable consideration. [851/508] An added condition on the sale was that the buyer pays all taxes due in 1934.

Registration post card for Labor Day 1933. (Betsy Camp)

1936

September, John G. Macdonald, a teacher and coach from Malden, managed the Ocean House bathhouse for the Camp family in the late 1930s during his summers off. His fun loving, witty, charismatic, and athletically talented son Torbert H. Macdonald entered Harvard University in 1936 and struck up a friendship with another student almost exactly the same age. They became roommates and later football teammates with Torbert serving as captain. So it was that John F. Kennedy occasionally came up to Short Sands with his roommate to visit family and play touch football on the beach with the Boardmans and the Ellises. The friendship lasted a lifetime, with Torbert serving as a groomsman in Kennedy's wedding; both as PT boat captains in the war; Jack as godfather to Torbert's son Torbert Jr.; and both in public service at the national level. (Reference: the November 17, 2013 edition of *Seacoast Sunday*.)

The yard in back of Ocean House c. 1936.
Left to right: Garages with laundry in the right end, boys' dormitory, girls' dormitory. (Betsy Camp)

MACDONALD FAMILY PHOTO/NFS

A photo from Torbert Macdonald Jr. of York, Maine, showing John F. Kennedy, left, and his father, Torbert Hart Macdonald, as roommates at Harvard University.

November 17, 2013 Seacoast Sunday. (Phil Meader)

1939

July 8, Season is off to a good start—Record year here is now predicted, *The Vacationist*

"If the crowd which gathered here at York over the holiday is any criterion of what lies ahead for the summer, this year should go down as one of the best in recent years. Veteran observers expressed the opinion that it was the largest gathering since the late twenties. Others went as far as saying that it was the biggest in 20 years.

"Whatever the actual number might have been, it is safe to say York's facilities were taxed and any more would have made free movement about the beach difficult. Automobiles filled up every available spot and spanned the boulevards in all directions. Despite the heavy influx of traffic, the local police handled the situation with admirable dexterity.

Short Sands Park across from Ocean House c. 1939. (Author's collection)

Ocean House and Short Sands Beach c. 1939. (Author's collection)

"Hotels and rooming houses, cottages and tourist camps were well filled with some places reporting full houses on the night before the Fourth. Guests at the hotels came from all parts of New England, New York, the South, Middle West and Canada.

"Trite as the expression may sound, none seems to express the tenor of vacationists here more than the old saw, 'A good time was had by all.' The 4th was celebrated in proper fashion. Fireworks, band concerts, baseball, swimming and fishing were the major attractions.

"This week-end the beach will return to its customary role as a delightful place in which to enjoy yourself. Your choice of relaxation is wide and somewhere here you will find that which meets your particular fancy. Sunday afternoon there will be a band concert at 2:30 and another in the evening at 7:30."

Bessie Fell Camp c. 1930. (Betsy Camp)

1940

September 3, *A Trans-Continental Journey from the Atlantic to the Pacific with the American Hotel Association,* a manuscript by Bessie Fell Camp, gives insight into hotel life and the personality of Fannie Ellis Simpson whose husband Willard managed the Ocean House during Frank Ellis's ownership:

"The summer usually ends for me when the Ocean House at York Beach, Maine, closes its doors the day after Labor Day. The summer of 1940 was no exception, but before we can depart for New Jersey, the hotel must be buttoned up for the winter. This heaving-to is a huge task, for it starts on the top floor, and goes down to the lowest basement. It turns the office into an accounting den; it makes good dispositions bad and bad disposition harder to live with. It is altogether the most disfiguring process I know. Between the cooking, the washing and ironing, the hammering and pounding, the whole place

is a noisy, steaming uproar of activity which gradually shuts out the daylight, does away with the hot water, wraps a winding sheet around the furniture, and hits the feather beds with a seasonal depression.

"One morning while this dismantling act was in progress, the telephone continued an incessant ringing. When Bess picked up the receiver, it was Lady Fannie Simpson of York Harbor who said:

"'Hello Bess that you?'

"'Yes, why hello Fannie, good morning.'

"'Still busy closing up, I suppose?'

"'You bet; right in the midst of the litter of summer. Didn't know I could accumulate as much trash in so short a time.'

"'Aren't you pretty tired, and don't you need a rest?'

"'Nothing I would like better, Fannie, but don't see how it could be managed with all that I still have to do.'

"'Well, I have a proposition to make, and you think it over. The A. H. A. are holding (their) annual convention this year in Seattle, Washington, and I have just been reading all about the trip and what they are to do, and where they are to go. It sounds simply wonderful and looks to me like the opportunity of a lifetime.'

"'Yes, I am sure it would be wonderful, Fannie, and I'd love to go, honest. But it would cost too much, and besides I couldn't be away very long anyhow.'

"'Now, I'm not going to keep you any longer, but you be thinking it over, and I'm coming over this evening and bring you the folder which tells all about it.'

"'Goodbye.'

"And that is how it started, and the following story is what came after, and where it finally ended.

"Lady Fannie Simpson is a very remarkable woman. She has owned and managed hotels for many years and all were efficiently run. She has a yen for management that took us all over the country in the front seat of busses, the best rooms in the best hotels, with the best price, and for the minimum cost. We got more for our money than any other three people on the trip, and I give the lady all the credit for her cleverness. Of course, I was managed, too, but as I no doubt needed it more than anything else, I profited by the experience.

"The trip really began on September 28 which was on a Saturday. It was a beautiful day which awoke the world with a hazy sunrise . . ."

1942

During World War II, F. Ellis Camp and his younger brother Paul B. Camp Jr., were both captains in the Army. Ellis was in the Signal Corps in the European conflict and Paul a

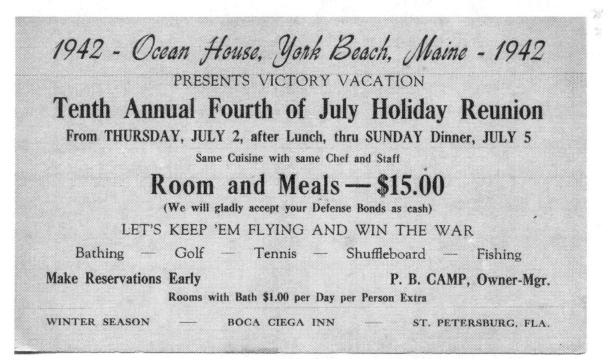

Wartime reservation card for the Fourth of July reunion. (Betsy Camp)

Flooding in the Short Sands Beach parking lot on August 26, 1946 after a 3–4 a.m. cloudburst. (Betsy Camp)

her in the hotel business. Ellis went to work for his parents in 1953 when Frank Parsons died, and Paul Jr., around 1955 when he built his house on Marietta Avenue. (2015 conversation with Betsy Camp)

1946

Flooding has long been a fact of life in downtown York Beach due to its low height above sea level. Historically, an open stream drained large marshy areas on both sides of Railroad Avenue to the ocean. Increasingly large penstock systems have been built to route this water to Short Sands Beach with the latest being completed in 2011.

ranger in the Pacific. After the war Ellis took a job in engineering at the Portsmouth Naval Shipyard so his wife Betty could be near her ill father in York Beach, Frank E. Parsons, and Paul majored in business and finance at the University of Alabama. Bessie Camp pleaded with her sons to come and work for

1947

In August a plan of land was drawn by Albert Moulton, C. E., for Paul and Bessie Camp showing the Ocean House property.

1948

June 3, A daughter, Elizabeth Helen Camp (called Beth), was born to Paul B. Jr. and Carolyn A. Camp.

July 3, A son, William Hunter Camp (called Billy), was born to Robert F. and Charlotte E. Camp.

September 15, A daughter, Beth Arlene Camp (called Betsy), was born to F. Ellis and Beth P. Camp (called Betty).

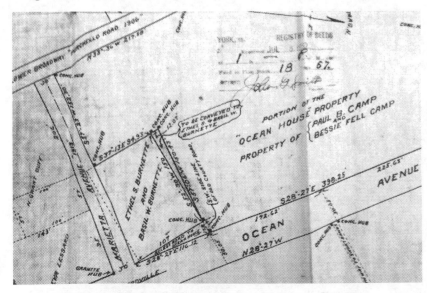

1951 Revision. ^{Plan 18/67} *(York County Registry of Deeds)*

1951

September 4, The Ocean House plan of land was revised to show conveyance of a triangular area between the York Manor and the Ocean House from Paul B. and Bessie F. Camp to Ethel S. and Basil W. Burnette. ^{Plan 18/67} This triangle of land was sold to the Burnettes to make the York Manor property more rectangular in shape again, and was roughly equal in size to a triangle lost on the other side due to changes to the layout of Marietta Avenue.

Bedroom suite looking into the turret above the front porch, 1952 brochure. (Phil Meader)

1952

The following is a composite of brochures (Betsy Camp and Phil Meader):

"Greetings from the Camp family to all for the 1952 season . . .

"A score of years ago Paul and Bess Camp took over the management of the Ocean House. During those years friendships have been formed and many dreams realized. There has been a steady improvement program in progress to give our friends more comfort, and better accommodations. Each year a new or different feature has been added to make Ocean House an attractive home for you during your vacation period. Last year the addition of the TELEVISION ROOM with its RCA 21" screen proved a never ending source of amusement all through the summer.

"This year, a new writing room is planned, on Mezzanine overlooking the dining room. Constant thought is being spent on how to build a better hotel, and how the small things which count can be introduced . . .

Television room, 1952 brochure. (Phil Meader)

MAIN LOBBY — OCEAN HOUSE, YORK BEACH, MAINE

"The interior of Ocean House is hospitable. A cheerful native rock fireplace greets the guest as one enters the lobby. A large picture window frames a seascape worth remembering. The dining room with a seating capacity of 175 overlooks the ocean. Fresh vegetables along with choice Maine lobsters, clams and seafood are features of the cuisine . . .

"Ocean House officially opens June 28th although the house will be in readiness to entertain early arrivals June 15th. The Motel, completed last season, will be open June 1st. It is now called 'THE SANDPIPER' and connection is being sought to affiliate it with QUALITY COURTS AND UNITED MOTOR COURTS. 'THE SANDPIPER' offers deluxe accommodations made comfortable even in the coldest weather by a central heating system, thermostatically controlled. Landscaping lends it the general appearance of the Hotel grounds . . .

"The Management continues to offer you the best of food, accommodations and service at the lowest possible cost. . . . We thank you, each and all, for your support in the past and appreciate your friendship and trust.

"THE CAMP FAMILY"

1954

March 25, Paul B. and Bessie Fell Camp conveyed the Ocean House property to their newly formed corporate entity Ocean House, Inc., for $1 and other valuable consideration.

This property included the Ocean House hotel, Seaford Cottage, two help's cottages, and New Annex as described in the April 12, 1934 deed from the Saco and Biddeford Savings Institution to Paul B. and Bessie F. Camp. [851/508] This deed excluded property conveyed by Paul and Bessie Camp to Lester M. Bragdon and

SANDPIPER MOTEL AT OCEAN HOUSE
YORK BEACH, MAINE
"Cross Lots from the Beach"

Sandpiper Motel rooms 1–5. (Betsy Camp)

then from Lester Bragdon to Bessie Fell Camp, Robert Fell Camp, F. Ellis Camp, and Paul B. Camp Jr. on September 26, 1951. A right of way which was established in the 1951 deed now crossed through the property transferred to Ocean House, Inc. in this 1954 deed. 1352/312

Another deed from Paul and Bessie to Ocean House, Inc. conveyed for $1 and other valuable consideration "All the furniture, fixtures, equipment, chattels, and personal property of every name, kind and description" associated with the properties just transferred. Still another deed transferred title to a 1950 Ford station wagon used for Ocean House business.

1955

September 26, Ocean House, Inc. sold a 100 x 100 square foot parcel of land to Paul B. Camp Jr. for $1 and other valuable consideration. This was on the north side of Marietta Avenue at the intersection with Broadway Extension. 1355/541 Paul Jr., constructed a house on this site facing Marietta Avenue and continued ownership through 1979 but lived in Florida full-time after the 1960 summer season.

November 4, When ownership of Short Sands Park was transferred to the York Beach Village Corporation on July 30, 1917 683/397, they were given the power to organize a board of trustees and adopt suitable by-laws for the protection, management, and improvement of the park. As the corporation had not organized a board of trustees and was managing the park by ordinance, a lawsuit had been initiated in 1954 by Alpheus D. Spiller et als., and on this date the state of Maine took action:

Ocean House c. 1954. (Author's collection)

"The Attorney General for the State of Maine, acting on behalf of the general public filed a motion for the appointment of Trustees for the protection, management and improvement of said 'Park' in accordance with said Deed of Trust . . ."

1956

January 3, The final decree was issued regarding the York Beach Village Corporation lawsuit by Cecil J. Siddall, Justice, Superior Court in Equity of York County (Case No. 1547).

House built by Paul B. Camp Jr. at the corner of Marietta Avenue and Broadway Extension. (David Pahl)

". . . WHEREFORE IT IS ORDERED, ADJUDGED AND DECREED:

"1. That said York Beach Village Corporation be perpetually enjoined from taking any action under said votes and ordinances.

"2. That the motion of the Attorney General for appointment of Trustees is hereby granted, and said Lawrence R. Ellis, Alpheus D. Spiller, Vincent D. Adjutant, John R. Garfield and Martin G. Chase, are hereby appointed and confirmed as Trustees of said "Park" with all and singular the duties, powers, discretions and subject to all conditions, confidences and contingencies set forth in said 1917 Deed of Trust to protect, manage and improve said "Park" in accordance with the terms of said deed.

"3. That no costs are awarded to any party hereto . . . " (from *Important Events in the History of Short Sands Park,*" March 24, 2011 published online by the Town of York)

Text from the 1956 Ocean House brochure:

"1956 Spring Greetings to All Friends . . . Summer memories! Happy days with easy informality at the seashore: sandy beaches, flying surf, rocky cliffs, sheltered coves. Weiner roasts, hiking to the Nubble, shuffleboard tournaments, the golden social hour before sunset and best of all, congenial people with whom to enjoy all.

"Since 1883 Ocean House, with its annex and cottages, has rested like a crown on the crest of a dune with a sweeping view of the majestic Atlantic and the rugged headlands which protect 'Short Sands.' For nearly a quarter century 'The Camps' have been greeting friends with a warm southern welcome on the long, wide, more than two hundred foot, veranda, three floors above the street level where the summer world passes in review. We deeply appreciated the

THE OCEAN HOUSE AND SAND PIPER MOTEL
York Beach, Maine

The aerial view on top shows Ocean House, Sandpiper Motel rooms 1–5 made from the former cement block garage with laundry on the right end, and rooms 6–11 at right angles to both. The bottom view shows a close-up of motel rooms 6–11 constructed new around 1955. (Betsy Camp)

cordial relationship which has existed for so many years between guest and management and express gratitude to all those who have spent their holidays and vacations at the Ocean House and have helped to make it a 'home away from home.'

"One of the spring projects is the beatification of the grounds in front of the Sandpiper Motel which is connected with the Ocean

Silver Jubilee brochure.(Betsy Camp)

House. Landscaping and an improved parking area will gladden the eye as well as being a convenience to both hotel and motel guests.

"Enclosed is the 1956 rate schedule with attached reservation request. Tentative reservations made last season should be confirmed by June 1st. June is a delightful month with special inducement of preseason rates.

"And may each of you, wherever you go, always find health, happiness and peace of mind.

"THE CAMP FAMILY"

1957

From the Silver Jubilee brochure:

"We Send You Maine and York Beach

"The OCEAN HOUSE with its face toward the sea, its arms outstretched in greeting; the warmth of a cheery fire in the lobby to welcome you when the nights are cool and the days sunny bright. YORK BEACH, a part of that New England where every man is neighbor to the sea and good food is a tradition. OCEAN HOUSE has atmosphere which is hard to describe for it has an undercurrent which is felt, but not visible. It springs from a desire to serve you, to surround you with little attentions, to make you comfortable and keep you happy . . .

"Yours in friendship, THE CAMP FAMILY"

1960

Paul B. Jr. and Ellis Camp, inside a room of the newly constructed Sandpiper Motel rooms 12, 14, 15, 16, and 17 on Broadway Extension, next door to Paul Jr.'s house, 1960. (Both, Betsy Camp)

The Camp family on the rear porch of the Ocean House dining room in 1960. Boys in front are, from left to right: Paul B. Camp III and Joseph Avery Camp (sons of Paul B. Jr. and Carolyn Camp)

All others, from left to right: Bessie Fell Camp; Paul B. Camp Sr.; Paul Jr.'s daughter Elizabeth Helen Camp (Beth); Paul B. Camp Jr.; Paul Jr.'s first wife Carolyn Camp; Franklin Ellis Camp (Ellis); Ellis's wife Beth Parsons Camp (Betty); Ellis's daughter Beth Arlene Camp (Betsy). Note the Willows cottage, upper right corner. (Betsy Camp)

Employee Stories

1961

Memories from Betsy Camp

Ellis Camp's daughter Betsy started working at Ocean House at age 13 in 1961 and continued to work there through the summer of 1976:

"Before 1961 the whole family would move to the Boca Ciega Inn in Gulfport, Florida for the winter season and to the Ocean House in York for the summer season. In Maine, Ellis Camp was in charge of overseeing the front desk, employee payroll, bills, etc. His younger brother, Paul Jr., was in charge of the kitchen, planning menus, ordering, etc.

Both Paul Jr. and Ellis could fill in either position—both were excellent chefs and bakers whether for one or 300 people. In Florida, Ellis and Paul Jr. reversed their roles.

"From a child's point of view, switching between hotels twice a year was very disruptive to school life. The school year started in York, transferred to Florida in November, and transferred back to York in April for the remainder of the year.

"Starting in 1961 Ellis and his family remained in York year-round and Paul B. Jr. and his family remained in Gulfport year-round. Paul B. Sr. continued to make the seasonal journey between the two. During the winter months Ellis, an engineer by training, would tutor York High School students in math, physics, and chemistry at all levels.

"April through June was the time for getting everything ready for the start of the summer season. It was the best day of all when the flag was raised for the first time, during the last weekend in June, signaling the hotel was open for business. The staff consisted of:

- 7 waitresses
- 1 side hall waitress
- 1 hostess
- 2 busboys
- 3 cooks, two for the guests, and one for the staff
- 1 baker
- 1 pantry, salad, and dessert person
- 1 pot washer/steward who also peeled potatoes and washed the kitchen floors with bleach nightly
- 1 steward's helper
- 2 dishwashers, one ran a cup and plate washer, and the other a glassware washer

Betsy, Ellis and unidentified clerk by the front desk with the candy, gum, and cigarette case under the stairs. (Betsy Camp)

- 1 houseman to support the chamber maids and bring linens to and from the laundry
- 1 laundry supervisor
- 3 chamber maids in the hotel
- 2 chamber maids in the 16 motel units and 2 cottages who also helped in the laundry
- 1 piano player during dinner, later an organist
- 1 night watchman
- 2 desk clerks
- 1 gardener

"The man who supervised and ran the laundry was an extremely strong African American named Major. He also served as bellman and houseman, and worked for the Camps for almost 40 years.

"The cooks, both African Americans, were Amos Lawson and Arbie (Brownie) Brown. Amos prepared the vegetables and worked

Amos Lawson and Ellis Camp in 1968. (Betsy Camp)

Four windowless basement rooms were located behind the large pine tree in this view. (Author's collection)

breakfast, lunch and dinner. Brownie prepared fish and meats, and worked lunch and dinner. The lunch and dinner menu was changed every day. Serving times were:

> Breakfast 7–9 a.m.
> Lunch noon–1 p.m.
> Dinner 6–8 p.m."

"Guests looked forward to picking up the evening menu at the candy counter by the front desk and before dinner filled out their own meal order form. Many of them were single or widowed women, and always sat at their favorite individual table, facing the ocean. The busboys would pass salad trays with a variety of jellied and fruit salads, lettuce, and relish trays with pickles, olives, carrot and celery sticks, and deviled eggs. All dressings were home made at Ocean House.

"There was one cook for the employees. His name was Vance Durrell, and his wife Archie Durrell was a chamber maid until age 85. When she broke her hip, she never revealed her correct age to Ellis, my Dad. Archie and Vance would travel with Paul Sr. and Bess from Maine to Florida. Paul Sr. and Bess owned a home in Belmar, NJ and they would stay there about two weeks, twice a year. Archie and Vance would do the cooking and cleaning for them."

"There were no days off until near the end of August when things slowed down. Two front desk clerks worked alternating shifts:

- 7 a.m. to 12 noon and 6–11 p.m. one day
- 12 noon to 6 p.m. the next day

"The African American kitchen employees lived underneath the northwest end of the hotel in window-less rooms. Segregation was still prevalent in early 1960s York. As unfair as it seems today, business owners had to maintain separate accommodations and it was not even possible for African Americans to rent housing in the York community.

"One year there were two gay waiters. This was still considered unusual around 1970, and there was a lot of talk behind their backs, especially among the older guests.

"Paul Camp Sr. was retired during this time, turning 80 in 1964, so he had no responsibilities other than to walk around and observe what was happening. He was a typical southern gentleman always dressed in a long sleeve white shirt, bow tie, and dark (usually

Paul B. and Bessie Camp on the left at Paul's 84th birthday party August 1, 1968, Betsy Camp on the far right. (Betsy Camp)

brown) trousers. Bessie Camp on the other hand was frequently writing letters and poetry to put in advertising brochures. She was quite the financial business woman who oversaw everything. She wore flowers in her hair and lots of costume jewelry, and was noted for her sewing, crocheting, and knitting. In Maine, she had her own bee hives for fresh honey on the tables. She was also the social butterfly and sat with all the ladies in the lobby before meal time."

"Once Paul Jr. remained in Gulfport, and was no longer available to share responsibilities at Ocean House, things changed. Ellis, my Dad, would get up very early every morning from the middle of June until the middle of September and work until 11:30 p.m. Betty, my mother, worked from 7 a.m. until 11:30 p.m. every day. Ellis was in the kitchen and Betty was at the front desk. Needless to say I didn't see them at home very often. Ellis handled the bills and payroll, and when needed, served as the electrician, plumber, and carpenter. Betty handled the reservations and correspondence, collected the guests' rent, and typed the menus which changed every day. Betty also oversaw the other two desk clerks to make certain that everything went smoothly and she was aware of the idiosyncrasies of each guest.

"In the dining room the clean white table cloths were changed two to three times per day as needed. The white linen napkins were folded in a particular way at each place setting. It was very formal, with two forks, a knife, two teaspoons, and one tablespoon. Beverages were placed above the knife and bread and butter plates above the forks. Meals were served to seated patrons from the right and taken away from the left.

Bessie Camp, on the left, and a beekeeping friend with her beehives out behind Ocean House. (Betsy Camp)

"There were always five choices for an appetizer (fruit cup, two soups, chowder, jellied consommé, etc.) Entrees consisted of haddock, beef, chicken, omelets, and about six different vegetables. For dessert there were sundaes, puddings, fruit, fresh sliced peaches and about five different pies. No alcohol was served except on Saturday. From 5–6 p.m. hors d'oeuvre and free alcoholic drinks were served in the lobby. Ocean House did not have a license to serve alcohol in the restaurant.

"After dinner many of the guests played cards. There were card party nights and the winner would receive a gift which generally came from the gift shop items that shuttled between the Boca Ciega and Ocean House. The Ocean House gift shop was called 'Witchcraft' and was located next door to the family owned Parsons Block in downtown York Beach. There were also bingo nights. Generally every night about 10 p.m. the dining room would open for fruit punch, cookies, cheese, and crackers.

Chefs Arbie Brown and Amos Lawson, Ellis Camp, and a waitress in uniform, 1967. (Betsy Camp)

"All waitresses wore white uniforms with white aprons and white shoes. Busboys wore white shirts, black ties and black slacks. It was very tasteful and formal. The chefs Brownie and Amos always looked great in their white starch uniform and white hats. They were really wonderful and worked for my Dad for many years until he had to close the dining room as it was too hard to find good help. One night the waitresses were complaining that they were so tired. It seems that after they served dinner at the Ocean House they would volunteer at a bar in town. Well, the night they complained to my Dad, he fired them all and told them to get off the premises. We got the busboys and chambermaids to serve the next day and no one knew anything happened.

"That was the last year he served three meals. Most guests had been on the American plan (with three meals a day provided) and had assigned tables. After this, breakfast was served Continental style with eggs, oatmeal, cereal,

toast, pancakes, bacon, etc., in the side hall near the kitchen. Whenever the dining room was in full operation it was opened to the public.

"My Mom and Dad were often so tired they just kept running on adrenalin. My Dad loved being his own boss and walking into the office and finding that all the rooms were taken. It was a great feeling for someone who tried so hard.

"Unusual things did happen though: One day he had to go into a woman's bedroom at the hotel as she was stuck in the bathtub. Ellis was tiny so he was able to get through the transom over the door and help the woman. One lady had a bedroom without a toilet, so she sat on the sink and broke it off the wall, causing water to come down into the dining room. Another woman was playing bingo and when she raised her hand to shout bingo she dropped dead. A 16 year old bellhop helped take care of her.

"The first Saturday in August the Ocean House always had a beautiful buffet with sterling silver trays, crystal, and all the staff dressed to the nines. After the dinner, the

The August 1965 variety show. (Betsy Camp)

Night watchman Charlie Markle and Betsy Camp in the office, 1973. (Betsy Camp)

'No Vacancy' sign. He practiced hospitality not found today; back then all the hotels and boarding houses worked together."

Memories from Peter Stanley:

"I was a House Man in 1964 when I was 17 years old, earning $35 a week. Job responsibilities included: sweeping the porch first thing every morning (it was a huge porch), helping the chamber maids and emptying their trash, vacuuming most of rugs in the entire place, and carrying the dirty laundry to Major in the laundry out back at the end of the Sandpiper motel. I then carried the clean laundry back to Vance Durrell's wife Archie where she would sort it, keep the best things for herself, and pass the rest along to the other two maids. Everything was spotlessly clean but some items were old and starting to show some wear. Victor Emmanuel, the piano player, was very elderly and stone deaf. He was a good piano player but occasionally had to be awakened so he would not sleep through dinner. He had a romantic

highlight of the evening was a variety show put on for all the guests by the employees. They even wrote an Ocean House song which became a traditional part of the show.

"On Saturdays all the women would dress in their long formal gowns for the cocktail party and dinner and then they would walk into town for shopping. As local author William Thompson said when the Ocean House closed 'the whole atmosphere in York Beach changed.'

"Charlie Markle was our last night watchman. He used to walk all the floors every hour to make sure everything and everyone was safe and secure and punch a clock at various sites.

"Ellis had a good rapport with other guest houses and hotels including the Wentworth on New Castle Island in New Hampshire, the Colony in Kennebunkport, and Cliff House in York, and if the Ocean House was full, the desk clerks would try to find lodging for anyone who inquired rather than post a

August 1964 chorus line from left to right: Peter Stanley, Patricia Keene, Dennis Reid, Tom Weinhold, Karen Avery, Mike Brown, Kathy Doyle, JoAnne Elms, Linda Ayres, Beverly Charrow, Diane Charrow, and Steve Harlow. (Betsy Camp)

1966, Dennis Reid, Mike Hunter, and Bill Furnas in the boys' dorm. (Betsy Camp)

interest in one of the guest's maids who was also very old.

"The next year I was a bus boy along with Dennis White from Florida. We did the heavy lifting for the waitresses, carried all the dirty dishes back to the dish washer, and carried the salads tray around to the guests. They could choose from canned fruit on lettuce, hearts of lettuce, or tomato aspic with 3 choices for salad dressing.

"The third season I went to summer school in Worcester and hitch hiked up to York every weekend and stayed in a spare bed in the boys' dorm. The last three weeks of August I was a waiter at the Algonquin restaurant where the Inn on the Blues place is now.

"The fourth summer I was a desk clerk at the Ocean House, handling all the money and billing, and supervising the bell hop. Betty was the boss and always pleasant to everyone. I did that for two years. There was a carpenter named Ed who ran the bathhouse, drove an Edsel Ford automobile, and did very little work that I could see in all the

years I was there. Once there was some real carpentry work needed and Ellis Camp did it with Ed as a helper.

"The sixth summer I had an engineering job at the New England High Carbon Wire Company in Millbury beside Worcester and drove to York every weekend and stayed in the dorm.

"We worked 7 days a week and never had a day off, but let's face it, we were at the beach in the summer and even a couple hours off was like a paid vacation. There were tips for occasional chores, when guests would request a favor or to carry, fix, or fetch something, averaging one or two dollars a week. That was enough to get by on. We had three meals a day and a room to sleep in provided so expenses were negligible. I came home at the end of the summer with every single pay check uncashed and put the entire amount in the bank.

"The last year, 1970, I was a bus boy and earned $15 a week because I was supposed to get tips from the guests. The tips were not that great until Labor Day weekend. With the place closing down the next day, many guests you had waited on the entire summer

1970, organist Russell Glynn playing the organ for the guests in the dining room. (Betsy Camp)

would slip you a five dollar bill or something, and at the end of that day my pockets were bursting with cash. Ever since then I have been a good tipper and wherever I get good service from a waiter or waitress I will give more than 20%, in cash if possible, and tell them 'put that in your pocket.' I know the feeling and appreciate a positive attitude.

"Ellis Camp was a wonderful boss, honest as the day was long, hard working, and would sometimes talk to himself as he usually had two or three projects going at the same time. He worked 16 hours most days during the summer."

Bathhouse Controversy

1965

July, Ocean House maintained a bathhouse next to the Short Sands Park boardwalk. The bathhouse was primarily for changing clothes and had no toilet facility, but did have an outside shower. Ellis Camp applied for a victualer's license so he could sell hot dogs along with the usual prepackaged food, soft drinks, and non-edible sundries to bathers at the bathhouse. This was approved by the York Beach Board of Overseers. The Short Sands Park Trustees, several of whom were restaurant owners, were not happy about this decision. They waited patiently until the first (and only) hot dog was sold at the bathhouse and took swift legal action to shut it down. (2014 conversation with Betsy Camp)

1966

October 12, **Parking In the Park,** *York County Coast Star,* editorial by A. B. B.:

"For a year and two months now we have followed a story in York Beach that had to do with the Short Sands Park Trustees and what appears to be their ultimate legal stalemate

of Ellis Camp and his operation of the Ocean House bathhouse and small-eats emporium. The bathhouse sits on a 100' × 100' square in the center of the park on a plot which the 1887 document recording the gift of the park land to the town euphemistically refers to as a 'pleasure ground' for hotel guests.

"We were content merely to report the news, what of it we could learn from officials, never until now taking an editorial stand. The issue was to be settled legally anyway. Ellis Camp operated the bathhouse-emporium and maintained the 8-foot path to it from the road in front of the hotel. There Camp sold prepared foods such as crackers and cookies, ice-cream, candy bar and tonic as well as non-edible sundries to bathers, mainly hotel patrons. This operation was inoffensive enough.

"The Park Trustees, however, had long fretted at the existence of this plot of privileged land. There it sat, at nearly dead center of their park, adulterating any comprehensive plan for harmonious park development.

"Then in late July last year Camp applied for a victualer's license from the Licensing Board. Camp wanted to serve hot dogs and perhaps hamburgers; he made no plans for remodeling or expanding. The Licensing Board granted him the license. The Park Trustees objected. The dispensing of the sundries and packaged items was one thing; a restaurant, in the middle of the park was another. They didn't really suspect Camp of future objectionable activity, but the granting of a victualer's license would set a precedent for all owners and all time.

"A local power struggle developed, accompanied by the hiring of legal advice. Tempers did not get out of hand, but it took a firm grip to keep them there. The public, meanwhile, looked on with somewhat less than partisan ferocity. The Park Trustees' attorney, Edwin Walker of Biddeford, ferreting around among the documents, came unexpectedly upon a modest piece of information that pretty well wound things up: Camp didn't own the piece after all, he said. Camp assumed he did, but he didn't. The Park Trustees sat back and loosened the rein. No need to be too heavy with the spurs now.

"The omission of a legally-required detail of ownership pretty much stifled all debate too. The editorial whose flowering we had awaited was snuffed out like a candle. There was no speech to make, and no light to read by. Privately we saw no harm in a hot dog or two and thought that if this would help Mr. Camp meet his competition by satisfying the odd wish of his bathers there were ways of permitting him to do so without opening the gates to all who followed. On the third hand we could not help but hope that soon the Trustees would be able to design a harmonious plan for the whole park at Short Sands. We assumed that they would want to maintain the airiness, the feeling of vista

from the street, the grasses, the sweep of the shore to the beach, to save that small strip of open land that lifts the center of York Beach out of what otherwise would be an ordinary cluster of commercial structures most of whose owners and lessees cater to tastes that must be termed no more than average for the vacationing American public.

"So when the Park Trustees finally were calling the turn, our twinge of regret for the misfortune of Ellis Camp was somewhat balanced by the assumption that the park would be saved, that one small strip of natural beauty in the center of York Beach was now safe from commercialism, perhaps forever.

"We were in for a bit of shock. This week the Park Trustees have permitted us to see and publish the Master Plan for Redevelopment of Short Sands Beach prepared by Wright, Pierce, Barnes and Wyman of Topsham. It looks as though the engineers and trustees were more concerned with commercialism in the area surrounding the park than in

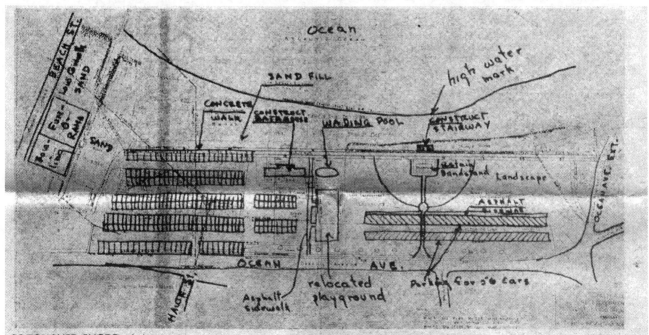

RE-TOUCHED PHOTO of the just-released Master Plan for redevelopment of the Short Sands Beach Park prepared for the York Beach Overseers and Park Trustees by Wright, Pierce, Barnes and Wyman, engineers. Cross-hatched areas are for parking cars. Concrete retaining walls to be built at the sand's edge, two sets of steps from it to the beach, asphalt walks and parking areas, a new bathhouse, relocation of playground, more seawall, a new wading pool, loaming and seeding for grass to replace dune grass, other landscaping, new sidewalks, curbs and other items are all parts of the plan.

maintaining the park in the spirit of the original gift, the spirit of natural beauty and open land, The view from most angles from the road to the water during the vacation season will be across expanse of blacktop, over the backs and through the windows of rows of parked cars.

"True, York Beach is short of parking space as it is short of park. It is also the opinion of the Overseers and Park Trustees that most people in York Beach think the major problem that the Short Sands Park can overcome is not a loss of attractiveness but a lack of increase in tourist convenience and are prepared to follow this public mandate by making the Park a park for cars instead of a park for people."

November 19, The Camps realized that the 1954 deed [1352/312] in which Paul B. Camp and Bessie Fell Camp conveyed the Ocean House property to Ocean House, Inc. did not include the 100 x 100 foot pleasure ground

across Route 1A directly in front of Ocean House as recorded in the Short Sands Park creation deed. A new deed was created which included the text describing the pleasure ground to make it clear that was a part of the Ocean House, Inc. holdings. [1744/370]

1967

March 9, **Snow Makes Its Weight Felt In York County,** *Portland Press Herald,* local news page:

"The recent storms which dropped heavy mantles of snow on York County have left their mark in the form of damaged and ruined buildings, two examples of which are shown . . . (seen here) is the Ocean House on Short Sands at York Beach where the heavy snow caused the collapse of a section of its porch. Police Chief James Morgan, Jr. said a motorist noticed the damage Tuesday . . ."

Bill Furnas performing in the dining room at Ocean House, August 1967. (Betsy Camp)

August 30, Innocent Verdict Given in Liquor 'Importing,' *Portsmouth Herald*:

"KITTERY—A York man was found innocent in Southern York District Court yesterday of importing more than a gallon of New Hampshire liquor into the State of Maine.

"Judge George D. Varney found William M. Furnas, 25, of Ocean House, York Beach, innocent of the charge after a hearing. Three other similar cases were continued to a later date."

"These were the first court cases brought in a crackdown against Maine residents buying liquor in neighboring New Hampshire and taking it across the state line. Furnas entered an innocent plea through his attorney, Robert J. Winton of York.

"Assistant Atty. Gen. Frederick P. O'Connell of Augusta, counsel for the State Liquor commission, prosecuted the case brought by William E. Gautreau, state liquor inspector. Gautreau testified that while maintaining a survey outside the state store on the Interstate Highway, Portsmouth, Aug. 25, he saw Furnas carry out two cartons and put them into a Maine car.

"He pursued the car across the Interstate Bridge into Maine and signaled Furnas to stop in a restaurant parking area. There he said he found Furnas had 18 fifths of whiskey and wine in the cartons, so took him to the Kittery police station.

"Gautreau testified that Furnas said he did not know it was against the law; that none was for himself, but some was for guests at the hotel and some for a cocktail party the hotel was planning. Furnas was then charged with importing more than one gallon of liquor, one gallon being allowable under the Constitution.

"Inspector Donald W. Lake testified that he observed the incident in New Hampshire while seated in a car a short distance from the store. He said he drove the car that pursued Furnas, also that he heard Gautreau advise Furnas of a 'transporting' charge and of his rights.

"Judge Varney supported Winton's contention the charge was premature since it was brought before the inspectors knew where the liquor was going. O'Connell pointed out that the charge could be amended even though he felt there was no difference between transporting into and importing. But he later said he would not amend the charge as it would be like 'double jeopardy.'

"Judge Varney found Furnas innocent saying the state fell 'far short' of proving the liquor was 'imported' illegally into Maine . . ."

1968

October 2, Judge H. Marden hears Camp vs. York Beach case; park bath-house decision to be made soon, *York County Coast Star*:

"The verdict lies in the limbo of Justice Harold C. Marden's secluded chambers in

Cropped aerial view showing the Ocean House bathhouse and shuffleboard court, 1944. (David Pahl)

Alfred, where the Superior Court Judge will weigh the attorneys' voluminous briefs, and make a decision after Nov. 1st. Meanwhile, the controversial bath-house continues to stand defiantly in the middle of York Beach (Short Sands Park), Park Trustees and Town officials cross their fingers, and Ocean House bath-house owner Ellis Camp sweats it out.

"The unusual story begins back in the stifling summer of 1965 . . .

"At that time, Aug. 26th and 27th, several York Beachers trooped to one of Alfred's Superior Court rooms, expecting to hear Judge Marden's final verdict. Instead, they heard more of the formal arguments by barristers Bragdon and Cyr, and testimony by two civil engineers, Park Trustee Edward Ellis, Overseer James Boardman, Paul Camp Sr., and Ellis Camp. York Beach Corporation Manager Ralph Blake was also present during the proceedings.

"Attorney Cyr explains that the term 'pleasure ground' referred to in the Ocean House deed is an euphemism for an abandoned croquet court across the street from the Ocean House, and that it is not a term interchangeable with "bath house", upon which the Camps have based their case. 'They are actually claiming rights to the bath-house on grounds of adverse possession (squatter's rights). This is a weird bird, and they are trying to establish a chain of possession for more than 40 years,' says Cyr. He also implies that it is very difficult for an individual to prove that his squatters' rights are valid when the land in question is actually public property.

"In any event, the case will not be decided until after Nov. 1st, when both attorneys will have submitted their final briefs to Judge Marden."

December 18, **York Beach bathhouse controversy settled by Supreme Court,** *York County Coast Star:*

"A controversy that has been raging for years was finally settled recently in York Beach when Maine Supreme Court Justice Harold C. Marden ruled that Ocean House, Inc. of York Beach has no legal claim to a frame structure in Short Sands Park known as the Bathhouse. The Bathhouse is a one story building, about 20' x 40', in the center of Short Sands Park. The Ocean House Hotel has maintained it for years as a private changing facility for its guests.

"For some years, the Trustees of Short Sands Park and the Town's Board of Overseers have tried to force the Ocean House to tear down the bathhouse so the park could be improved and developed. The Ocean House claimed it had a right to the land the bathhouse stood on according to the terms of an 1887 deed which set up the entire tract of beach in front of the Ocean House Hotel as a public recreation area, but set aside a 100 square foot area as a 'pleasure area' for the hotel guests. The Ocean House maintained that the bathhouse was within this 'pleasure area.'

"The Trustees of the Park ordered the Ocean House to remove the structure in 1966 and as a result, the Ocean House, Inc. filed a petition for a declaratory judgment to determine the ownership of the bathhouse. Recently Justice Marden handed down his judgment. He ruled that the 1887 deed, in fact, did give the Ocean House a right to a 100' x 100' pleasure area, but that in the terms of the deed, and in other documents, this area was placed in different locations. He found, however, that the piece of land the Hotel claimed bordered on Ocean Avenue, running 50 feet to either side of the sidewalk from the hotel to the bathhouse. Since the bathhouse is more than 100 feet from the street, then, Marden ruled it was not within the limits of Ocean House, Inc. jurisdiction. He said that the Ocean House had failed to prove a right to the bathhouse either by adverse possession or by grant."

DISPUTED BATHHOUSE, once belonging to Ocean House, Inc., now the property of Short Sands Park Trustees.

"Having suddenly found themselves with a bathhouse, the Trustees of Short Sands Park have not yet decided what to do with it. Corporation Manager Ralph Blake indicated that the Trustees might not meet until January, but when they do, it is expected they will arrange to have the bathhouse torn down."

1971

The public bathroom in front of the Bowling concession was upgraded by the Trustees of Short Sands Park. That building was replaced with a brand new facility in 2014.

Three Years of Change

1973

June 15, Robert Fell Camp, the oldest son of Paul B. and Bessie Fell Camp, died at age 58. During World War II Robert was employed by the Boeing Aircraft Company and later the Winchester Repeating Arms Co. After World War II he worked for The Boston Wire Stitcher Co., which became Bostitch, Inc., in 1948. Later he owned a highly successful industrial stapling business. He was not involved in either of the family's hotel operations.

September 20, Boca Ciega Inn—New ideas for old hotel location—Would 34 apartments be better than this empty hotel? *Gulfport Gabber*

"Boca Ciega Inn, the eye-sore of Gulfport, according to city officials and residents, may be replaced with a 34 unit apartment building if the elected city officials will re-zone the 2.4 acre tract at 31st Avenue and 54th Street South.

"Two potential buyers of the site appeared before Gulfport City Council at their work session meeting, Thursday, September 13th, to get the feelings of council as to the possibilities of a variance rezoning or whatever might be required to construct their proposed building.

"Gulfport has established an R-4 zoning area for high-rise buildings in the Town Shores of Gulfport section. Boca Ciega Inn is in an R-3 zone and will not permit construction of a building 75 feet high, the height required for 6 stories of living units plus parking under the building.

"To qualify for flood insurance the first floor of a building must be 12 feet above the ground (on the water front) the reason for this type of parking arrangement.

"Gulfport's density ordinance will permit 15 living units per acre. Part of the 2.4 acre tract is submerged land, but according to the proposed buyers, the site will meet all requirements of city ordinances in its present zoning classification except for the height.

"City Manager Tony Harwig told the investors that he would recommend, to council, not to give a variance explaining that they

Boca Ciega Hotel has been called a "Fire Trap".

could apply for a variance or rezoning. He did not say he would or would not recommend rezoning.

"The only positive indication by members of council was that they would like to see the Boca Ciega Inn replaced. Estimates on removing the one time thriving establishment is between 10 and 16 thousand dollars, council was told.

"The interested couple said a contract for purchase is subject to a variance or rezoning to meet their needs."

1974

February 14, **The Death of Dignity,** *St. Petersburg Independent*:

"The glory days pass and all that remains is shattered windows, a weed-filled yard, a rusty beer can in a foyer where men and women once lifted elegant cocktail glasses. Gulfport's Boca Ciega Inn, built during the boom of the 1920s, is soon to die. The old building, which nudges Boca Ciega Bay at 54th Street and 31st Avenue S and was once a popular winter resort, is expected to be torn down about the middle of March. The old resort was closed in 1970; since, it has been battered by vandals and used as a hiding place for derelicts and lovers."

April 4, **Boca Ciega Inn—53 years from vacant lot to vacant lot,** *Gulfport Gabber*

"The winter home of millionaires for over 40 years, Boca Ciega Inn has been demolished, making room for an apartment complex at 54th Street and 31st Avenue South, Gulfport.

"The Inn, built in 1921–22, was leased in 1931 by Paul B. Camp for 1-year with an option to purchase. Camps purchased the facility which included 4 lots for $32,500. The furnishings cost another $2,500. This covered furnishings for 40 sleeping rooms plus kitchen and dining room furnishings.

"During later years, the Camp family purchased an adjoining lot to become the Bait House area and the cost was $6,500.

"Paul B. Camp Jr. said the resort was opened only seasonal, about 6 months a year. After the war the Inn was open from November–April.

St. Petersburg Independent, *staff photo by Ricardo Ferro.*

Paul Camp Jr. took over the operation of the Inn in 1951 and closed the doors in 1970.

"Mr. and Mrs. Paul B. Camp Sr., at the age of 88 and 85, are residents of Gulfport. Their son said his parents made the guest list at the Boca Ciega Inn grow from 10 when they took over, to a full house every season with 95% rented for the following season before closing date.

"Camp said that a million dollars in the 30s, 40s, and 50s represented a lot of money and there were few millionaires during those early years. The owners recall that for about 20 years the Boca Ciega Inn was the winter home for 7 to 10 millionaires."

"The one-time ultra resort was sold in 1971 for $66,000. The Bait House and lot sold for $38,000 last month. The Inn never reopened as a hotel after 1970. Camp Jr. said he sold the property for $105,000 what cost his parents $39,000 when the buildings were but 10 years old."

The variance required by the new owners was not approved, so the apartment complex was never built.

December 5, P. B. Camp, 90, owned resort inn, St. Petersburg Times, obituary:

"Paul B. Camp, 90, retired owner of the Boca Ciega Inn, 3126 54th St. S, Gulfport, died Wednesday (Dec. 4, 1974).

"The inn was built during the boom of the 1920s and was operated by Mr. Camp from 1932 to 1970. It was torn down this year. He also was the owner of Ocean House Hotel in York Beach, Maine from 1932 to 1970.

"A resident of 5202 26th Ave. S, Gulfport, Mr. Camp was born in Sulphur Springs, Tex., and came here 49 years ago from Jonesboro, Ga. He was a graduate of Gordon Military Institute, Milledgeville, Ga.

"Survivors include two sons, Paul B. Jr., Gulfport, and Franklin E., York Beach,

Paul B. Camp Sr., in 1962. (Betsy Camp)

Maine; six grandchildren, and six great-grandchildren. . . ."

1975

January 16, Bessie Fell Camp died at age 86, less than six weeks after her husband.

1976

December 13, Betty Parsons Camp and her sister Martha Parsons Colletti of St. Petersburg, Florida sold the Parsons Block next door to the Kearsarge/Shelton Building on Railroad Avenue to Ernest S. and Eleni Paras of Wells, Maine. [2162/640] Betty, who was doing all the reservations and correspondence for the Ocean House hotel, was battling cancer by this time and as a result she and Ellis started scaling back their responsibilities.

December 30, A one-third interest in the Ocean House Motel and Cottages was transferred from the estate of Bessie Fell Camp to Franklin E. Camp. The executors of the estate were Paul B. Camp, Jr., and lawyer Malcolm B. Arthur II, both of St. Petersburg, FL. [2228/94] The motel and cottages were operated separately from the affairs of Ocean House, Inc.

On the same day Paul B. Camp, Jr. conveyed his one-third interest in the land and buildings known as Ocean House Motel 1 through 5 to Franklin E. Camp for $1. [2229/25]

1977

July 21, Ellis Camp doing business as Ocean House, Inc. sold the Ocean House property to Orbust, Inc. A seasonal parking lot and three rental cottages, C, D, and E adjacent to the Ocean House and behind the Cavanaugh cottage, remained under Ocean House, Inc. ownership. Ellis had purchased rental cottages A, B, and C and moved them from a location near the VFW Hall on Cape Neddick Road. During the off-seasons he added two rooms to cottage C and built cottages D and E from scratch out in back of the Cavanaugh house.

Although Ellis worked far more hours in the family hotel business than if he had stayed in engineering, he enjoyed being his own boss and using his talents as carpenter, painter, wall paper installer, electrician, and plumber in running and maintaining the hotel. (2015 conversation with Betsy Camp)

Ellis Camp c. 1990 (Betsy Camp)

Epilogue

June 26, 1984, Betty (Parsons) Camp, Ellis's wife, died at age 64.

May 27, 1991, Franklin Ellis Camp died at age 73. Ownership of Ocean House, Inc. was left to his daughter Betsy Camp who continues to manage the parking lot and cottages C, D, and E in 2015.

March 25, 1995, Paul Benjamin Camp Jr., died at age 72, leaving his ex-wives Carolyn and Colleen, three children, and seven grandchildren.

July 4, 1997, Gulfport Veterans Memorial Park was dedicated on the former site of the Boca Ciega Inn. The site, which was cleared in 1974, was never developed due to denial of a height variance needed to make an economically viable high rise.

CHAPTER 3

Rivers Family/Orbust, Inc. Ownership

The Early Years

1977

On July 21 Orbust, Inc. purchased the Ocean House property from Ocean House, Inc.

The new owners of Ocean House faced headwinds of change and regulation: the era of large service oriented hotels with well-heeled long term guests had passed; the third floor was closed off due to requirements for an expensive sprinkler installation.

July 13, **A York Beach landmark changes hands—Hotel opens with energy,** *York County Coast Star*

"Turn of the century luxury summer resorts on the ocean have become but a memory of plush velvet drapes, high ceilings, fashionable dining, and wealthy patrons sitting on long walking porches in seersucker suits drinking mint juleps. But today a small part of that memory is alive in York Beach, reborn with the restoration of The Ocean House, one of those old-time elegant hotels.

"Although the atmosphere has become more casual and it is no longer for the elite only, The Ocean House features bell-hops, the porch, and the furnishings of an era thought to be forgotten.

Don Rivers, general manager of the hotel and a member of Orbust Inc., entered into the hotel-restaurant endeavor "with absolutely no experience."

linens, renovate the kitchen, fix the driveway and then open on the 24th of June.

"The men—Don Corsen, Bob, Dave and Don Rivers—have 'never had any experience in either the hotel or restaurant business' but do not consider that a handicap. 'We've done

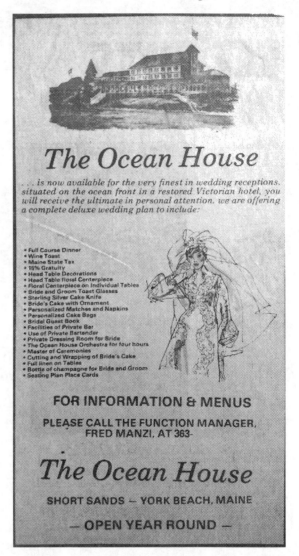

Newspaper ad (Museums of Old York) Fred Manzi, a barber and musician in Arlington, MA, worked on the side at Cottage Crest Restaurant in Waltham doing weddings and functions. Don Rivers, also from Arlington, asked Fred to help out at Ocean House as function manager. Ads like this one attracted some clients, but customers were often disappointed due to the inadequate facilities, especially the heating system.
(2014 Conversation with Fred Manzi)

"Five weeks ago, the hotel changed owners. For the past 44 years, Mr. and Mrs. Franklin Camp of York Beach owned, operated and personalized the service of Ocean House. But with the increasing demands for labor and cash to keep the hotel overlooking Short Sands Beach operating, the Camps realized the demands were more than they could meet reasonably.

"Although the new owners have been 'planning this all winter,' the four men from Massachusetts who formed Orbust Incorporated to operate the Ocean House did not close the deal until five weeks ago. Three brothers and a close friend who claim 'having our summer roots at York Beach for more than 35 years' arrived in early June to paint ceilings, fix plumbing, paint dining room furniture, hire a 45-member staff, replace it to try it,' says Don Rivers, formerly a data processing consultant with Children's Hospital in Boston. 'I have great hopes but it all depends on this summer. We've pooled all our resources and hope to have a really nice thing here.' he adds, providing an explanation for the name of their corporation—Or bust.

"Wishing to continue 'the quality service' theme the former owners established for the hotel, the new owners are attempting to mix new ideas with the tradition already established. Don Rivers, whose father still lives in York Beach year round and whose grandfather operated the bath houses at the Beach, calls The Ocean House 'a landmark.'

"According to the general manager, the original building of the existing hotel served the public as a roller-skating rink in 1862 [1884]. The floor of the right hand lobby where patrons may now sit and play cards or have cocktails is the original oak and herringbone patterned one the skaters used. In 1884 [about 1885], the two story section housing the rink underwent renovations including a three-story addition and was converted into a hotel.

"'There's a lot of sentimental attachment to this place,' explains Rivers with no small amount of enthusiasm and animation. 'We plan to restore the hotel rooms to about the time of 50 years ago. Every room is different and will remain that way,' he says of the 90 unit hotel part of his adventure.

"While much has been done in the five weeks Orbust, Inc. has operated The Ocean House, more is expected to be done within the year. 'We plan on staying open all winter, if we can,' says Rivers. 'Because we are working under limited time conditions we can't do everything right away.' But hopefully during the fall and winter, the company of four will replace the roof, the asbestos shingles with cedar shakes and most importantly, install a heating system. The hotel has never had anything more 'than the space heater you see in the corner,' laughs Rivers pointing to a corner in the dining room.

"Rivers' bearded face breaks into a quick grin as he talks about the future. 'Let's just forget we don't have any money.' According to his brother Bob, the winter nights of planning were spent 'pretending we had a million dollars. But we are always trying something new, trying to do something as an alternative to spending money we don't have.'

"Operating a hotel or a restaurant alone presents a multitude of problems from customer satisfaction to fixing leaking pipes, but with a building as old as The Ocean House the problems are compounded.

"'Well, first of all we had to get all the licenses a place like this requires,' begins Rivers about to use his fingers to indicate each step. 'We needed an eating and lodging, a shellfish, a dancing, the entertainment, a victualer's license . . . I think there are more. We didn't really need the dancing, but I said why not after all the other applications.

"'The biggest problem is that we don't know what to expect—how much food to buy,' he continues. 'The breakfast had taken off but the dinner dining room hours are just gearing up.'

"According to the Accommodations Host Frank Luppine, the Ocean House was 'always a place people around here came to have breakfast. With all the other things we had to do, we had no time for any advertising so our breakfasts are busy.' Breakfast, available for the working man beginning at 7:30 a.m., is served on the porch overlooking the ocean, in the coffee shop attached to the kitchen or in the formal dining room.

"Other problems, according to Rivers, have included the plumbing; the dishwasher ran without water and burned out the heating coil, a resident raccoon that likes 'to run across the porch and the problem of the day—what is proper dress?' Today we had that question come up. 'What do you say? What do you do? Got any suggestions?' and he laughs.

"Coping with problems Rivers has never experienced before has a special trick, according to the general manager. 'The trick is not to get overwhelmed by any one thing.' He attributes a great deal of his flexibility to the 'wonderful cooperation and willing help from the Camps. They weren't willing to sell this place to just anybody, and they've been very good to us. He lives near here and when we call, he is always ready to help.'

"Keeping with the innovative spirit Orbust, Inc. promotes, this weekend saw the first sing-along. 'Many of our guests have come here for 40 years or more. With the younger crowd that has been attracted this year, we wondered how everyone would mix. We have a piano player (who also plays through the dinner hours) and decided to start a happy hour from 4 to 6 each afternoon. This afternoon people came in from the porch to sing and it was great.'

"The music, like the atmosphere, had something to offer for both the young and old who to Rivers surprise, 'thinks what we are doing here is great. One woman said it was great to see young people around like this.'

"Orbust, Inc. has decided to add a word to the original name of this 'once very elegant hotel.' According to Rivers, 'We've added "The" to Ocean House because we think it is special.'

"Rivers, who has moved to the area year round and who will be joined by his partners within the year, feels the hotel has a role in the community. 'York Beach is a family beach. It is in the middle both physically and in atmosphere of Hampton Beach and Ogunquit. I think something like this will swing it the right way, maybe helping it from getting too much of any one thing. By restoring The Ocean House, I think we can save a part of the Beach.'"

July 21, The legal transfer of property from Ocean House, Inc. to Orbust, Inc. included the following properties:

- For $1 and other valuable consideration, the 100 x 100 foot "pleasure ground" on the north side of Route 1A directly in front of Ocean House. [2230/99]

- For $10,000, Ocean House, Inc. agreed to sell at a later date a parcel of land behind Ocean House previously owned by Richard and Ingrid Boardman, and described here on the Moulton Engineering Co. Plan of Land [Plan 86/18] as Lot #4. [2230/101]

- For consideration paid, the Ocean House property described here on the Moulton Engineering Co. Plan of Land Plan [86/18] as Lot #2. [2230/104]

- On the same day Orbust, Inc. granted a 15½ year mortgage for $230,000 at 8% annual interest to Ocean House, Inc. using the Ocean House properties described above as collateral. This instrument was signed by Donald P. Rivers as treasurer of Orbust. [2230/108]

1978

August 18, Orbust, Inc. granted a second mortgage to the Small Business Administration on the Ocean House property to secure payment of a $277,600 promissory note. [2401/205] The mortgage was signed by David F. Rivers as president and Donald P. Rivers as treasurer for Orbust, Inc.

September 20, **Nostalgia is alive and well at York Beach Ocean House,** by Leonard Witt, York County Bureau, *Portland Press Herald:*

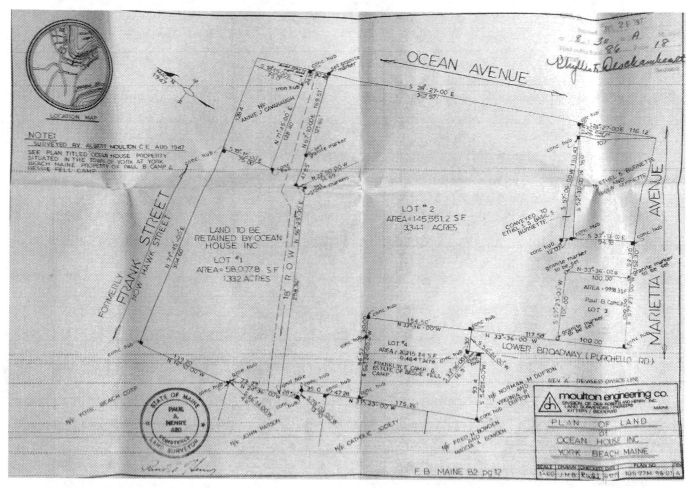

Moulton Engineering Co. Plan 86/18 updated for Ocean House, Inc. in June 1977 (York County Registry of Deeds)

"YORK—Only his mustache provides a clue that Donald Rivers might be interested in nostalgia. It is well-groomed and curls at the ends, just like the ones you see in old-time photographs.

"Of course, there's another clue—a bit larger one—that he and his three partners have deep feeling for the good old days: the Ocean House at York Beach.

"The hotel was born in the days of the grand Victorian hotels. The Ocean House was not so grand as most of its era, however. In fact it was first established as a roller skating rink back in 1862 [1884]. Later, the hotel was built around the rink.

"Like most Victorian hotels, it had its good years. But after the war, it began to fall into disrepair.

Donald Rivers at the Ocean House. (Witt Photo)

"Rivers and his brothers, David and Robert Rivers, and partner Donald Corson formed Orbust, Inc. more than a year ago to save the old hotel.

"Rivers says all four were doing well in other businesses but wanted to invest in something else, and that something else turned out to be the Ocean House.

"'When we bought it was so run down you wouldn't believe it,' Rivers recalls. 'It had gloomy hallways and dark rooms.'

"A Massachusetts architect was hired, and the Rivers brothers and Corson began renovating the hotel.

"'We could have torn it down and built a motel for a lot less,' Rivers notes. But he adds, 'If we were to tear it down and put up a modern motel, then what's next for the town? I'd hate to see York Beach go down the tubes, because it's such a nice town.'

"To improve the appearance of the hotel, the four partners ripped off the asbestos siding and repainted the exterior. But the most impressive renovations were made inside the hotel.

"Part of the second floor was ripped out above the dining room, and skylights were built into the roof. Now the dining room is

The interior has been renovated, with skylights lending a light and airy atmosphere to once dark and gloomy areas.

light and airy, and 14 rooms that were once hidden down dark corridors now encircle an indoor veranda overlooking the dining areas.

"Someday the men hope to build small shops below the hotel, and they have plans to build an indoor pool. They are also preparing to put in year-round heating to keep the hotel open this winter. They hope to obtain income from having weddings and other functions at the hotel.

"In the meantime, there is a lot of work to be done. Only 14 of the 84 units in the hotel proper and small motel units in the rear have been renovated.

"But already there is quite a difference. A guest, Peter Ryan of Waltham, Mass., says he had come to York Beach often but until this year would never have stayed at the hotel. He says it was run down and adds that, in general, he is a 'motel person.' But this year he tried the Ocean House.

"'This is quite a transition,' he says. 'I like the no telephones, no television and I like the convenience.'

"But Ryan, who is a building contractor, says he's not sure Rivers and his partners can make a go of the Ocean House. "'It's hard to bring one of these places back,' he says. 'It's quite a challenge and will take a lot of money.'

"But Rivers says he and his partners are confident of success. 'It will work out,' he insists. 'There is no question about it. It's tripled its value since we bought it.'

"But he admits it has cost him some gray hairs, a receding hair line and about 20 pounds so far. He still maintains he and his partners did the right thing.

"'We're getting a whole new crowd of people,' he says of the hotel's guests. He says today (they) rarely stay in hotels, and the Ocean House is a novelty to them. Unlike at motels, people can sit around in the lobby of a hotel, go to the lounge to have a drink or sit on the porch and meet new people.

"During the summer, there was jazz on the hotel porch and this fall he plans ballroom dancing.

"'The thing is to try to get as many things going as possible so you attract a wider range of people,' he says.

"So far, older guests have returned for repeat visits and more and more young guests are staying at the Ocean House, he says. That may mean that grand old hotels—like mustaches—may be coming back in style."

The Ocean House had a successful year the summer before the sale to Orbust, Inc. even though the third floor had been closed off in lieu of installing an expensive sprinkler system to comply with fire regulations. Knowing the level of hard work and care that went into maintaining Ocean House as a showplace for satisfied summer guests, it was difficult for the Camp family to read the characterization "When we bought it was so run down you wouldn't believe it," in the article above. (2014 conversation with Betsy Camp)

1979

July 13, Orbust, Inc. borrowed an additional $275,800 from the Small Business Administration. Since the property was already heavily mortgaged, additional items were included as security for this loan:

"Together with and including all buildings, all fixtures including but not limited to all

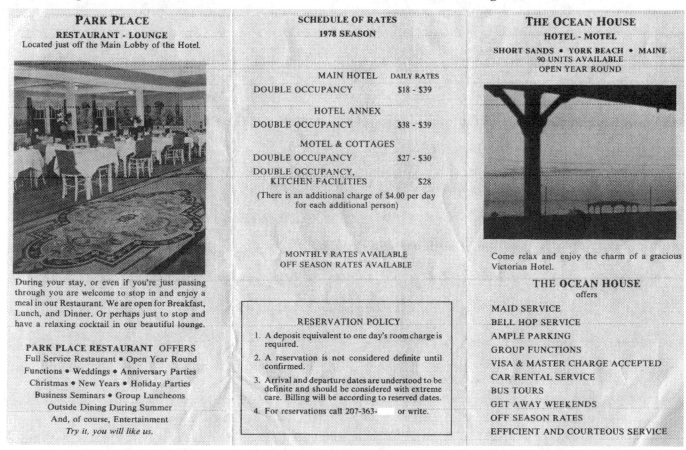

Brochure: Promising a full service year-round restaurant and hotel-motel with 90 units available for the 1978 season. (Betsy Camp)

plumbing, heating, lighting, ventilating, refrigerating, incinerating, air conditioning apparatus, and elevators (the mortgagor hereby declaring that it is intending that the items herein enumerated shall be deemed to have been permanently installed as part of the realty), and all improvements now or hereafter existing thereon . . ."

The new loan amount, not including interest, totaled $553,400. The document was signed by David F. Rivers as president and Donald P. Rivers as treasurer for Orbust, Inc. [2401/205]

October 16, Two corrective deeds and a land transaction were recorded on this day:

- Deed [3526/302] added a detailed description of Ocean House Motel 1-5 land conveyed from Paul B. Camp Jr. and Malcolm B. Arthur II to Franklin E. Camp in a December 30, 1976 deed. [2201/60]

- Deed [3526/306] added title references to the deed conveying a former Lester M. Bragdon lot from Franklin E. Camp to Ocean House, Inc. dated July 21, 1977. [2229/25]

- Deed [3533/172] completed the transfer of Lot #4 behind Ocean House previously owned by Richard and Ingrid Boardman, as agreed to in the July 21, 1977 deed. [2230/101] Signed by president Franklin E. Camp for Ocean House, Inc.

November 19, Martha F. Gordon conveyed two parcels of land, located between Short Sands Park and Ocean Avenue Extension, to the Town of York under the control of the Trustees of Short Sands Park for "One Dollar and other valuable considerations." There were restrictions: "The land herein conveyed is to be forever used and occupied by the public for a 'Park' and is not to be enclosed by a fence or wall of any description and is to be forever under the management and control of the Trustees of Short Sands Park." This is essentially the same language used in the original deed to create the Park. [2595/244]

Financial Woes and Time Shares

1980

March 11, The Maine Employment Security Commission filed a lien against Orbust, Inc. for $91.04. Document signed by Assistant Attorney General Leon V. Walker Jr. [2627/217]

March 17, The Maine Employment Security Commission filed another lien against Orbust, Inc. for $4,200.22. Document also signed by Assistant Attorney General Leon V. Walker Jr. [2627/218]

April 16, The Town of York filed a tax lien on Ocean House for $5,551.54. Document signed by Rega A. Bridges, Tax Collector for York. [2648/217]

July 30, A writ of attachment was issued on behalf of Joseph A. Arendt, against Orbust, Inc. doing business as The Ocean House, in the amount of $11,500. [2680/320]

September 4, The U.S. Government filed a Federal Tax lien against Orbust, Inc. for $31,241.45. Document signed by William R. Laidley, Revenue Officer. [2694/294]

1981

August 4, The U.S. Government released the September 4, 1980 Federal Tax Lien with balance left of $1,554. 50. Document signed by John T. Moran, Advisor / Reviewer. [2829/19]

The flyer on the right shows that Orbust was promising a full service restaurant, year round operation, a venue for functions, weddings and parties, and entertainment. (Note that the construction dates, 1860 for the roller skating rink and 1872 for the hotel, are incorrect.)

While striving to run the hotel as promised in their flyer, Orbust, Inc. was also promoting the pre-sale of timeshare units at The Ocean House by posting an announcement in newspapers and mailing out the following

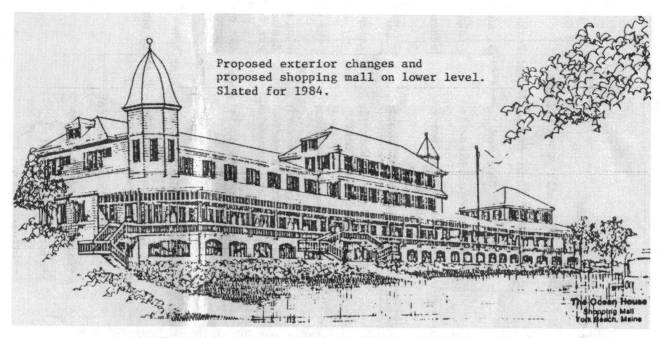

Proposed exterior changes and
proposed shopping mall on lower level.
Slated for 1984.

1981 Proposal for a shopping mall underneath Ocean House. (Betsy Camp)

PARK PLACE

RESTAURANT - LOUNGE
Located just off the Main Lobby of the Hotel.

During your stay, or even if you're just passing through you are welcome to stop in and enjoy a meal in our Restaurant. We are open for Breakfast, Lunch, and Dinner. Or perhaps just to stop and have a relaxing cocktail in our beautiful lounge.

PARK PLACE RESTAURANT OFFERS
Full Service Restaurant • Open Year Round
Functions • Weddings • Anniversary Parties
Christmas • New Years • Holiday Parties
Business Seminars • Group Luncheons
Outside Dining During Summer
And, of course, Entertainment
Try it, you will like us.

1981
RATE SCHEDULE

	DBL	SGL
Mezzanine	53.00	45.00
Room w/full bath	38.00	32.00
Room w/half bath	30.00	25.00
Room without private bath	27.00	22.00
MOTEL UNIT	38.00	32.00

****
*Extra person in room $5.00 per day (under 12 yrs. free with parents)
*10% discount on weekly rentals
*20% discount on monthly rentals
*Family special (up to 5 people) $199. tax included for five nites (motel units only)

Check out time   11:00 AM
Check in time   2:00 PM

RESERVATION POLICY

1. A deposit equivalent to one day's room charge is required.

2. A reservation is not considered definite until confirmed.

3. Arrival and departure dates are understood to be definite and should be considered with extreme care. Billing will be according to reserved dates.

4. For reservations call 207-363-   or write.

By 1888 we were 28 years old.

The building was originally constructed as a rollerskating rink in the year 1860. Approximately 12 years later the 3 story section with 35 sleeping rooms was erected. Since then the building has served as a hotel, with a calm, relaxing atmosphere allowing you to feel completely at home.

Our front office staff is prepared to handle the individual traveler, the large tour or convention. We are a year round hotel situated back approximately 100 yards from the surf with literally miles of sandy beach right outside our front door. We are within walking distance of all activities yet far enough away to be quiet.

Promoting the 1981 season. (Betsy Camp)

prospectus to interested parties (both, Betsy Camp):

"TIMESHARING AT THE OCEAN HOUSE

"Thank you for your interest. We are attaching information on the exciting concept of timesharing which we hope you will find both informative and stimulating. We are also taking this opportunity to tell you about the York Beach area which is considered New England's most beautiful seacoast resort area.

"The owners and management of THE OCEAN HOUSE have made a commitment to convert the inn to a time-shared resort. News travels fast! While not officially ready to begin sales, many knowledgeable people have expressed an interest and desire to become part of the program at ground floor level.

Announcement: The Ocean House is now a Time-Shared Resort. (Betsy Camp)

"The owners and managers of THE OCEAN HOUSE have authorized us, GALTEE, LTD., their marketing representatives to begin a Pre-Sale Program. We will be pleased to show you how it works and how you will benefit.

"THE OCEAN HOUSE will retain its distinctive Victorian elegance. After all we are enjoying over 125 years of history in this splendid building. All changes will be made with the Victorian theme as paramount consideration. Changes! There will be many and they will be constant over the next several years.

"The first of these changes is happening now. We invite you to inspect our model rooms in King Arthur's Court which is on the mezzanine level above the atrium. All rooms will be furnished and maintained in the same high quality as you will find in the Sir Lancelot (230) and Queen Guinevere (229) rooms. This high quality and attention to detail will be contractually guaranteed each and every year thereafter through a regular schedule of redecoration and refurbishing. We will initially be offering 35 rooms and 4 suites with a completion date of April 1982. Each section of the building will enjoy a distinctive theme with the rooms being named appropriately to the theme. For example, on the 'Authors' level there will be the Longfellow Room. On the 'Mariners' level there will be a John Paul Jones Room.

"THE OCEAN HOUSE is being offered to you as a timeshared project from the middle of April through the first week of November thereby giving you the finest seasons to select for your vacation time. You may want a week in the spring for golfing, two weeks in the summer for the beach, and a week in the fall for the foliage. THE OCEAN HOUSE can meet every vacation need and every budget. We look forward to helping you select your vacation with us. SEE YOU AT THE OCEAN HOUSE.

"GALTEE, LTD., 189 Campbell Avenue, West Haven, CT 06516"

June 15, The York Sewer District filed a lien against Orbust, Inc. for $2,373.29. Document signed by sewer district treasurer Walter E. Webster. [2809/205]

1982

August 21, Edward M. Ellis, a grandson of Frank Ellis and long-time trustee of Short Sands Park passed away. The Short Sands Park Board of Trustees were advised by their attorney that a name change could be done, and voted at their November 1982 meeting to change the name to Ellis Park in memory of Edward and to honor the family whose generosity and foresight had created the park in 1887. The new name was engraved into entrance pillars at the west and south entrances that were added as part of a park improvement plan (2014 conversation with Bill Burnham).

October 1, In the U.S. District Court, a complaint of foreclosure was brought against Orbust, Inc. on behalf of the following parties: Connecticut National Bank; Town of York; York Sewer District; State of Maine Department of Manpower Affairs; Joseph Arendt; Robert Memory; Thomas Fierro, and Fred James. The document was signed by Deputy Clerk Constance E. Wilde of the United States District Court. [2988/26] Mortgages involved were:

- Original SBA mortgage for $277,600 dated August 18, 1978 [2401/205]

- Increased SBA mortgage totaling $553,400 dated July 13, 1979 [2537/107]

West entrance to Ellis Park. (by Author, 2007)

October 23, **Ocean House gets sued by the federal government,** by staff writer Pam O'Neil, *Portsmouth Herald*:

"YORK—The United States government has filed a civil suit against the owners of a 125-year old York beach hotel—the Ocean House.

"Filed in U.S. District Court in Portland on behalf of the Small Business Administration, the suit asks the court's permission to foreclose on the Ocean House mortgages, unless the owner pays some $665,000 owed on promissory notes and interest.

"Besides naming Orbust, Inc., the Augusta corporation that owns the hotel, the suit names the Town of York, the York Sewer

YORK OCEAN HOUSE

District, and the State of Maine—all holders of liens on the property.

"Also named are a Connecticut Bank, one Connecticut and two Massachusetts residents, and a Portland firm.

"All of those named must file an answer within 20 days.

"The block-long, wood frame hotel located on Ocean Avenue across from Short Sands Park, was most recently being developed by Orbust as a 35-room, four-suite time-share resort.

"Scheduled for completion in April 1982, the resort was offering long-term leases to prospective vacationers.

"In August 1978, Orbust president David Rivers and corporation officer Myron Rust signed a promissory note to the SBA for $277,600. The mortgage was registered on Aug. 22, 1978.

"In July 1979, they signed for an additional $275,800 increasing the amount owed to $553,400. That second transaction with a revised interest rate and a new monthly payment of $3,012 was dated Sept. 15, 1979. As collateral, they put up all the hotel's furniture, fixtures, equipment and machinery.

"In its suit, the federal government charges that Orbust is in default on the first promissory note, the additional attachment to it, both mortgages, and both security agreements.

"Orbust has paid nothing toward installments since September of 1979 with the result that the corporation owes the government $569,332 in principal and, to date, additional interest of $95,851, increasing at the daily rate of $78 a day.

"The government therefore claims it is entitled to foreclose on both mortgages and to have a United States marshal or his deputy sell the land and premises and apply the proceeds to pay amounts due.

"The government also asks that Orbust pay any deficiency in funds that may exist after such a sale.

"The town of York is involved in the suit because it filed a $6,903 lien on the Ocean House property for unpaid 1981 property taxes and interest.

"The Sewer District has filed liens for unpaid sewer bills.

"And the State Department of Manpower Affairs has filed seven liens against Orbust for unpaid unemployment taxes for the period from March 1979 to March 1981.

"Others named are the Connecticut National Bank; Joseph Arendt of Stow, Mass.; Robert Memory of South Attleboro, Mass.; Thomas Guarto Ferro of Wallingford, Conn.; And Fred S. James & Co. of Maine."

Condominiums

1983

June 22, Condos on tap for Ocean House resort, *York Weekly*:

"Plans are being formulated to build condominiums in back of the Ocean House Hotel overlooking Short Sands beach, according to one of the owners of the historic development.

"Donald Rivers, one of the partners in Orbust, Inc., the owners of the hotel, said he and his partners are in the process of reorganizing their corporation to bring in new money to finance the demolition of the structure behind the hotel and build in excess of 50 . . . first class condominiums.

"Rivers said once the financing is worked out and the plan receives the town's approval, construction should begin sometime this fall.

"While the condo plans are in the works, Rivers said the hotel will be opened on the weekend of July 4. He said the delay in opening has been caused by his recent illness. Rivers further stated that he and his partners 'will honor' time sharing agreements purchased with customers previously.

"In a related matter, Orbust is still involved in a court suit with the federal Small Business Administration for allegedly failing to pay back $665,000 in loans and interest borrowed from the SBA in 1978 and 1979 to finance their original modernization plans.

"The SBA is attempting to foreclose on the hotel in an effort to recoup the money Orbust supposedly owes. Orbust also allegedly owes money to the town of York, the York Sewer District, and the state of Maine.

"Rivers said the new plans for the structure should not be affected by the lawsuit 'because any action we take' to improve the facility and earn revenue will be looked upon with favor by the SBA and the other litigants."

During this time of Orbust financial trouble some banks became confused between "Orbust, Inc. doing business as The Ocean House" and "Ocean House, Inc." Ellis Camp's bank accounts were attached several times, but eventually the error would be cleared up and the bank would apologize (2014 conversation with Betsy Camp).

September 2, A survey of the boundaries of Ellis Park (formerly Short Sands Park),

The Ocean House resort hotel overlooking Short Sands beach in York Beach could include condominiums by next year.   *Photo by Michael Burns*

across the street from Ocean House, was prepared by John P. R. Cyr, Maine Registered Land Surveyor, of H. I. & E. C. Jordan, Surveyors (a division of Edward C. Jordan Co., Inc. of Portland, Maine). This survey brought together very diverse information—historic stream locations, former parcel boundaries relating to the Buswell and Gordon donations, the location of the use easement held by the Ocean House, approximate utility locations, four historic layouts of Ocean Avenue along and through the Park, and deed references for properties shown on the plan. Plan 125/13 (Plan is not shown here.)

1984

July 17, Relative to the October 1, 1982 complaint above, the attachment of the real estate of Orbust, Inc. doing business as The Ocean House is dissolved and discharged. Document signed by Richard G. Moon, Attorney for Joseph A. Arendt. [2533/152]

November 28, **The proud past of the Ocean House,** by Laurie Ledgard, *York Weekly*:

"Ocean House, oh how we love you
With your view so fine
Set beside the sea so blue
Never leave our mind

"Verse from song written by former Ocean House employee in 1950s.

"It was not so long ago when the staff of the Ocean House would sing the words to this song during the annual show at the end of the summer season. Nor was it long ago that elegantly-attired men and women, guests of the old hotel, would gather at five in the afternoon for cocktails before being ushered to the dining room for dinner.

"And, not too long ago, waiters and chambermaids dressed in crisp, starched uniforms to perform the services necessary for the preparation of the Ocean House.

"Franklin Camp recalled all this and more about the hotel his father first leased in 1932 and then bought a year later [the purchase was completed in 1934]. In 1977, Camp sold the hotel and an era ended. But not the memories.

The Ocean House staff performing the annual show in 1964.
(Betsy Camp)

"While sifting through the memorabilia collected in his desk, Camp found a postcard showing the dining room of the hotel as it once was. A fine Persian rug, once belonging to the president of Woolworth's, Camp said, graced the old floor beneath it where roller skaters once danced. The chair backs were orange, he said, to match the orange in the carpet.

"'That carpet cost $18,000 in 1932 and it weighed a ton and a half.' Camp remembered this week. 'I left it in the dining room when I sold the hotel. I understand the roof leaks now. This is the way it looked when I sold it,' he said, pointing to the postcard.

"The dining room had a 10-foot balcony where a small band of musicians would play while guests were being served. Camp said the wall paper in the dining room, which seemed to show small pastoral settings with graceful old trees, was bought from a guest of the hotel who taught Camp how to hang it.

"When Camp ran the Ocean House, he said dressing for dinner was not just a treat, it was a necessity. There were no bathing suits or bare feet allowed in the dining room. And only in the last 10 years of the hotel did he allow women to wear slacks to dinner.

"'I kept the dignity of the hotel up,' he said.

"Deep inside the drawers of another desk, Camp found some photographs he took before the hotel was sold. Each photo showed one of the many sofas or tables that Camp said he found for the hotel at auctions and flea markets, and then reupholstered. Some of the pieces he said he kept. Others, he left in the hotel for the new owners.

"A former guest of the hotel gave Camp an old wooden piggy bank, shaped like a barrel with a copy of a woodcut of the

Woolworth executive's rug purchased for the Ocean House dining room. (Author's collection)

Ocean House dining room with wallpaper and balcony c. 1942. (Author's collection)

Ladies' lounge June 28, 1976 by Ellis Camp.

Lobby June 28, 1976 by Ellis Camp.

Ladies' lounge June 28, 1978 by Ellis Camp.

Ocean House on one side. Camp believes the old bank may have been bought or given as a gift in the late 1800s.

"The memories of his days as the hotel's proprietor include the bad times or, at least, the tough times. Camp recalled the winter day when 200 pieces of linen were frozen solid after he tried to take them by truckload to be laundered.

"So gone now is the elegance, the panache, the 'je ne sais quoi' that gave the Ocean House its own unique place in the memories of York Beach residents and visitors, alike. The era of summer finery and frocks, where Glen Miller music might have drifted from the hotel onto the beach below, while guests dance on the veranda is, perhaps, gone forever.

"Memories we'll carry with us
When we head for home
Of your guests that do befriend us
By the sea and foam"

November 28, Drainage still a concern to neighbors, by Laurie Ledgard, *York Weekly*:

"Many York Beach residents who live on the streets surrounding the Ocean House property attended the public hearing held two weeks ago to hear discussion on the plans to transform the 127-year-old hotel into condominiums, complete with restaurant and swimming pools. Some of those residents told members of the York Planning Board of their concern over proper drainage for the property because of the flooding they see each spring. That concern has not left them.

"'I recognize that they can't leave it as it is, they have to do something with it,' said Rex VanAken, a Marietta Road home-owner. Though he believes the property

A REAR VIEW of The Ocean House, where 22 townhouse units have been proposed for construction by the Spencer Group.

needs redevelopment, VanAken is concerned about drainage.

"Standing outside on the rear deck of his neat gray split-level home, VanAken described the flow of water each spring from the hills on property behind his house.

"VanAken said his concern was that if the Ocean House property was built up two feet as proposed, water would be flowing onto his property from two directions: the hill behind his house and the Ocean House in front.

"'I'm concerned about building in York,' he said. 'Is the water supply adequate enough to support this (project)? It seems some studies ought to be done.'

"VanAken and his wife Shirley said they were both worried about traffic congestion in the area, particularly in the summer. Residents who live in the summer homes on adjacent streets often use Marietta Road to travel back and forth to Short Sands Beach. The proposed plans for redevelopment show that cars will be forced to exit the rear of the property onto Marietta Road, and the VanAkens are concerned about the additional traffic and the numbers of children who play in the area.

"Among other things in the proposed plan, Richard Wiggin said he felt there were too many townhouse units planned for the rear of the hotel. Proof of that, he said, was that the developers did not have enough space for proper setbacks, which was a concern of the Planning board at the subdivision review two weeks ago.

"Wiggin also raised drainage problems discussed at the public hearing. 'I've been here for 64 years and everything they said is true,' he said. 'That parking area out front has had three to four feet of water on it, part of the back-up of the drainage system and the ocean. It's pretty hard to add to a system that's already full.'

"'I'm not against it, I'm against them doing things wrong,' Wiggin continued. 'The variances they want shouldn't be allowed. There's a lack of parking and there's going to be a big traffic jam problem in the back. They'll have a problem when it snows. They won't be able to get plows in and they'll have to shovel by hand.'

"Wiggin said he believes the only solution to the drainage problems in this area would be a whole new drainage system, yet, he said, that conversion should not take place 'unless the town makes a bigger system. Why should the people pay extra taxes to drain the Ocean House?'

"Richard Wiggin's twin brother Raymond is a resident of nearby Church Street. He agrees there are too many townhouse units proposed for the property.

"'I think they're trying to build too much in too small an area. I don't think the size of the property goes along with the zoning laws. It was obvious at the (planning board) meeting that they couldn't meet the zoning laws,' Raymond Wiggin Said. 'They can't build as many units as they propose to build. It

The lowlands under discussion behind Ocean House. (David Pahl)

would be no benefit to the town and it would disrupt the whole area.'

"Franklin Camp owned the Ocean House hotel after his father Paul B. Camp Sr., first bought the hotel in 1933 [1934]. Franklin Camp now lives on Church Street, right behind the Ocean House. Drainage was also his primary concern about the proposed project.

"'There is 3.34 acres of land there. If they come up two feet, that's going to give them 6.68 acres or 45,000 square feet,' Camp said during an interview at his home. 'Multiply that out and figure the number of gallons of water that could be out there. About 570,000 gallons of water. Now, what's going to happen with only one foot of pressure to push that water to the ocean? The business section of York Beach will be flooded out. I'm more worried about that than anything else.'

"Many of those who spoke at the Ocean House public hearing recalled the wrath of the winter storm of 1978 that brought flooding to most of the New England coastline, including York Beach and the Ocean House area. Camp said—less disastrous storms in 1946 and 1953 also brought flooding to the area.

"'I don't see how they can do it. I may be wrong,' Camp said.

"Of the project as a whole, Camp said, 'As far as I'm concerned, if they can get drainage and sewerage, I don't have any problems with it. I don't think the beach is ready for it. I may be wrong. I personally think they're trying to crowd too much into too small an area.'

"Plans to convert the old hotel into condominiums were first brought to the attention of the planning board in July of this year. The present owner, Orbust, Inc. bought the property from Franklin Camp in 1977. The Orbust corporation was suspended in 1983 after failing to file an annual report with the state of Maine and was threatened with takeover by the federal government for nonpayment of more than $15,000 in back taxes.

"The plans for redevelopment by the Spencer Group of Newton Highlands, Massachusetts were explained to the public at a hearing Oct. 15. The plans include a series of townhouses in the rear of the main building, condominium units in the hotel, retail space, a restaurant and pub, and two swimming pools."

1985

April 18, The Harold F. Udell plan for Ocean House was approved by the Planning Board of York, Maine and was recorded in the York County Registry of Deeds on May 14, 1985. Plan 137/4

May 9, The Maine Department of Labor, Bureau of Employment Security partially discharges multiple tax liens against Orbust recorded from February 25, 1979 to November 15, 1984. This document was signed by Stephen Sargent as Chief of Tax. 3533/135

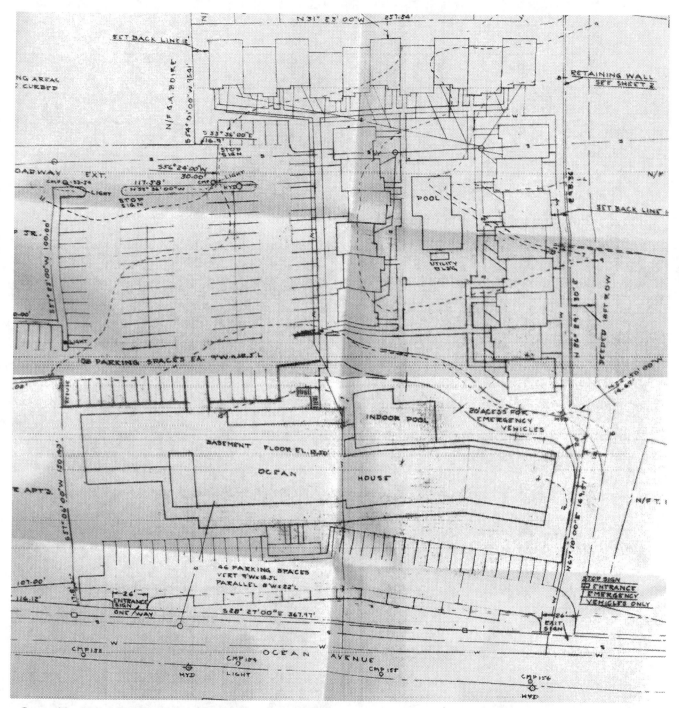

Created by Harold F. Udell, P. E., for Orbust and developer Spencer Group in 1984. In January 1985 it was updated to reflect the new developer, Seabury Housing Associates. Plan 137/4 *(York County Registry of Deeds)*

May 22, Ocean House, Inc. releases land and buildings to Orbust, Inc. for consideration paid. Signed by Franklin E. Camp as president of Ocean House, Inc. [3533/153] Land is described in the following documents:

Parcel A: Ocean House, Inc. to Orbust, Inc. first parcel dated 21 July 1977. [2230/104]

Parcel B:

- Bragdon to F. Ellis Camp, right of way dated 26 September 1951. [1192/395]
- Boardman to Ocean House, Inc., water line easement dated 6 July 1961. [1460/205]
- Ocean House, Inc. to Orbust, Inc. dated 21 July 1977. [2230/101]

Parcel C: Ocean House, Inc. to Orbust, Inc., second parcel dated 21 July 1977 [2230/104]

Parcel D: Access road between Ocean Avenue and Burnette property

Easement A: Ocean House, Inc. to Orbust, Inc. easement dated 21 July 1977 [2230/104]

Easement B: Ocean House, Inc. to Orbust, Inc. "Pleasure Ground" dated 21 July 1977 [2230/99]

Additional references:

- Case of Ocean House, Inc. versus James Peck et al., Civil Action Docket 9456.
- Plan for Ellis Park by H. I. and E. C. Jordan dated August 1983. [Plan 125/12]
- Plan of Ocean House, Inc. by Moulton Eng. Co. dated 17 June 1977. [Plan 86/18]

May 28, The Small Business Administration, with Thomas A. McGillicuddy signing, discharged the following interests: [3533/159]

- Mortgage from Orbust dated 18 August 1978. [2401/205]
- Mortgage from Orbust dated 13 July 1979. [2537/107]
- York Sewer District liens dated 17 May 1982. [2924/10]

Epilogue

2013

July 4, 2013, The Fred Manzi Trio played their last concert at the Ellis Short Sands Park gazebo. Fred Manzi, the unpaid Ocean House function manager during the Orbust, Inc. era and a resident of York, officially retired from musical performance in December. (2014 conversation with Fred Manzi)

November 25, 2013, Don Rivers of Rivers by the Sea LLC, and the project developer for the Atlantic House at York Beach, filed for a Chapter 7 voluntary bankruptcy petition in the U.S. Bankruptcy Court in Portland. (Reference: Seacoastonline.com September 23, 2014 article by Susan Morse)

2014

September 23, 2014, Article by Susan Morse, Seacoastonline.com:

"YORK—Don Rivers, once head of one of the largest summer rental businesses in York, the developer who was key to what was called the 'renaissance' of York Beach, is looking to clear his name and get back in business.

"At 67 and facing personal bankruptcy, he has to get back in the game if for no other reason than financial survival. While the bankruptcy involves dozens of creditors in the seven figures and threatens to take the Ocean Avenue Extension home he has shared with his wife Mary Rivers for 30 years, it

Don Rivers (Rich Beauchesne, Seacoastonline.com)

does not affect his long-standing real estate business, Rivers By the Sea.

"'I want my 300 customers back,' Rivers said from porch of his 100-year-old yellow beach cottage.

"To do that, Rivers must salvage a reputation damaged in a financial slide that claimed the Atlantic House, Kearsarge House and Rock-A-Way Inn in York Beach, along with at least a dozen homes.

"Vendors and other creditors, brides who had booked their wedding receptions, and renters who paid deposits for summer vacation homes but arrived to find them not available, all lost money . . .

"Rivers feels a camaraderie with Artie T. [DeMoulas], he said, because Arthur S.'s sisters, Diana Merriam and Fotene DeMoulas, were the biggest investors in the Atlantic House, the centerpiece of Rivers' envisioned renaissance for a year-round York Beach.

"It opened late in 2007 and included condominium/hotel units on the third and fourth floors, the restaurant Blue Sky on York Beach on the second, and retail shops on the first . . .

Atlantic House under reconstruction, June 17, 2007. (by Author)

"The DeMoulas sisters loaned him about $5 million for the estimated $8 million Atlantic House project, Rivers said. They did so after seeing a sign hanging over the yet-to-be-renovated building that said, 'Good luck Don,' according to Rivers, who said both women have summer homes in York.

"The sisters, through their company Lawrence Investment Holding LLC of Boston, held the mortgage to the eight hotel/condominium units, according to Rivers. In January 2012, the hotel condominiums were sold at auction to Lawrence Investment Holding, the single entity that expressed an interest in buying the units.

"As D & D Management, with a shared Park Plaza address as Lawrence Investment Holding, Merriam and DeMoulas held Blue Sky and Clara's Cupcake Cafe on the first floor, under the name Two Beach Street.

"'We controlled the operation, they controlled the money,' Rivers said. 'We couldn't make a move without them.'

"In April 2012, a York County Sheriff evicted Rivers from Blue Sky and Clara's Cupcake Cafe for failure to pay close to $20,000. Rivers said he had stopped paying the money in January because he believed he and the DeMoulas sisters were about to work out a deal that would have allowed him to buy back the hotel and keep Blue Sky . . .

"However, their attorney Tom Fitzpatrick, president and managing partner of Davis, Malm & D'Agostine, P.C. in Boston, said the sisters, through their companies, went out of their way to financially help Don and Mary Rivers. The couple was in default of payments since 2010, Fitzpatrick said.

"For Don Rivers to try and say, 'Diana Merriam pulled the rug out from under

The closed Blue Sky Restaurant at left, September 2, 2012. (by Author)

me, it's an outrageously untrue statement,' he said.

"'Back in 2007 they provided a great lot of money in financing to the Rivers, including mortgage loans, buying and then renting restaurant equipment and a promissory note for their own personal funding of their business,' Fitzpatrick said. 'The Rivers and their businesses were unable to live up to the obligations that were governed by those contractual arrangements.'

"From April through Oct 2012, negotiations between the sisters and Rivers ensued, but they never were able to come to terms on an agreement, he said.

"'We spent a tremendous amount of time trying to be responsive to these proposals,' Fitzpatrick said.

"The money owed totaled more than $20,000, Fitzpatrick said. According to the figure on the Rivers' bankruptcy records, they owed the sisters' business entities at least $120,000, Fitzpatrick said.

"Another investor complicating the mix was Darryl McCauley, half brother of comedian Dane Cook, who invested $2 million in the Atlantic House, according to Rivers. McCauley was later convicted of stealing $11 million from Cook during his time as business manager for the comedian. His wife Erika McCauley was also charged.

"In December 2008, York police were among the authorities who seized more than $800,000 from Darryl and Erika McCauley's condo at the Ocean House, another Rivers development. Erika McCauley had also invested in two commercial condos on the first floor of the Atlantic House.

"Rivers said he was as shocked as anyone else when he learned of Darryl and Erika McCauley's arrest.

"In a letter dated June 16, 2009, Attorney George 'Toby' Dilworth of Portland, representing Cook, demanded Rivers return funds invested by the McCauleys in the Atlantic House, according to court documents.

"Rivers replied to Dilworth by e-mail the next day, June 17, according to court records, saying, 'This is absolutely the most (ridiculous) request I have ever received. As far as I'm concerned I have dealt with what I believed to be a reputable family for over 20 years.'

"The Atlantic House hotel has since reopened and Blue Sky is run under new management as Gigi's . . ."

CHAPTER 4

Robert Dunfey Jr./Seabury Housing Associates

1985

May 29, Orbust, Inc. with David F. Rivers signing as president, conveyed the Ocean House properties to Seabury Housing Associates for consideration paid: [3533/175]

Ocean House, now owned by Seabury Housing Associates, in summer 1985. (Betsy Camp)

The Ocean House, fenced off for construction. (David Pahl)

- Parcels A and B and Easement A conveyed with Warranty Covenants.
- Parcels C and D and Easement B conveyed with Quitclaim Covenants.

September 21, Ocean House won't be destroyed, by staff writer Pam O'Neil, *Portsmouth Herald*:

"YORK—The very ground under the Ocean House trembled this week as word got around that a licensed engineer has pronounced the building unsafe, in danger of collapse, and eligible to be torn down immediately.

"But the developers deny there are any plans to destroy the old York Beach hotel.

"Meanwhile the Planning Board wants to be sure the building is going to be rehabilitated rather than reproduced, since approval of the project was based on that understanding.

"The issue arose less than a week before Seabury Associates, the group about to start converting the old hotel into 43 condominiums, is scheduled to break ground at the Ocean Avenue site across from Short Sands Beach.

"The Sept. 12 letter from state licensed engineer Robert Nason recommending demolition reached York Town Hall this past Wednesday.

"Questioning Seabury President Robert Dunfey and architect Warren Freedenfeld about it, Town Planner Tony Dater was told nothing of the sort was going to happen. And those assurances were quickly followed by a memo from their contractor Donalco of Portland.

"Donalco outlined the construction schedule:

- The hotel will be divided into segments which will be temporarily moved and stored on another part of the site while the new foundation is being built.

- As soon as the foundation is ready, the building will be erected using as much of the existing structure as possible.

"Former York Code Officer Armand Tremblay told the Planning Board Thursday night that the developers' intent has always been to preserve the Ocean House.

Backhoe removing porches around the north sleeping wing. (David Pahl)

"They've merely found some new structural problems that must be addressed, he said. But they're willing to accept the increased cost.

"New Code Officer Bob Davis, who spent hours inside and under the building this week, said many of its main beams have been cut and its timbers broken.

"And Davis told the board that he wants to continue investigating to determine whether the building should actually be condemned as unsafe and demolished . . ."

Groundbreaking

September 22, **Ocean House groundbreaking Tuesday**, *Portsmouth Herald*:

"YORK—Gov. Joseph Brennan will host groundbreaking ceremonies Tuesday at 10:30 a.m. that begins the reconstruction of the Ocean House on the shores of Short Sands Beach in the heart of York Beach.

"It will be building into 43 luxury condominium units, each overlooking the ocean. Built more than a century ago, the landmark resort will be the centerpiece of a multi-million dollar condominium project of Seabury Housing Associates.

"According to Robert J. Dunfey Jr., Seabury's president, 23 luxury townhouses will also be added to the site. Work on the main building begins this week, and project coordinator Donald Rivers of York Beach said some units will be ready for occupancy next summer . . ."

Exposed underpinnings of the north sleeping wing. (David Pahl)

September 25, **Ocean House called symbol of progress**, *York Weekly*:

"Governor Joseph Brennan, the guest of honor at the Ocean House groundbreaking ceremony Tuesday morning, shoveling a small clump of dirt near the front steps of the former resort hotel, a York Beach landmark which will be rebuilt into 43 luxury condominium units by Seabury Housing Associates.

September 24, groundbreaking ceremony, Robert Dunfey Jr. at the podium next to Governor Brennan, Don Rivers to right of the project display board. (David Pahl)

ROBERT DUNFEY, JR., left, the president of Seabury Housing Associates which is developing the Ocean House, and Governor Joseph Brennan officially marked the start of the century-old hotel's renovation on Tuesday morning.
Photo by Dean Rock

"'The Ocean House has long been a landmark to visitors to Maine. Its renovation is a symbol of progress for York Beach and a tribute to the quality of life in Maine,' Brennan said to observers gathered in a tent erected across Ocean Avenue from the building, which was built over 120 years ago. Such a revitalization, he said, 'creates a new sense of pride in the community.'

"Robert Dunfey Jr., president of Seabury Housing Associates, said he became involved with the Ocean House project because it 'saved the architectural integrity of this unique landmark structure,' which was for

A backhoe brings down the New Annex. (David Pahl)

many years the 'focal point' of resort life in York Beach. Dunfey thanked many people, including town officials, for being 'very supportive' and planning board members for reviewing the project may times over the course of a year before granting approval.

"Dunfey said he was unsure how much of the existing building would be used in the construction process, which he estimated would be complete in 12 to 13 months, but said he was meeting after the ceremony with town planner Tony Dater, code enforcement officer Robert Davis, administrative assistant Donald Cole, the architects, and the contractor, Donalco, Inc. of South Portland, to 'come to common ground' with respect to 'what components can be used in the new building.' Ann Reiss, an architectural historian with the Old York Historical Society has been asked to attend the meeting as well.

"'It's going to be a more beautiful building,' stated Dunfey, who said the plan to increase the length of the building will 'make it more dramatic,' Each of the 43 condominium units in the main building will have 'unobstructed ocean views,' according to Dunfey, who said skylights and cathedral ceilings would be standard features for these units and for 23 two-bedroom units to be located behind the main structure. Dunfey added that 'extensive landscaping would also enhance the project.'

"This week CEO Davis will conclude an investigation of the structure to insure safe working conditions and the 'safety of the building when it is completed.' Davis said he hopes the developers will be able to 'use as much of the existing building as humanly possible.'

"'We need to put piling underneath there in order to have a foundation that's going to work and that's going to be sound,' said Dunfey, noting that this would

Burning of demolition debris with the York Beach Fire Department standing by. (David Pahl)

require moving the building. Dunfey said an engineer confirmed that the building 'is not structurally sound.'

"Donald Rivers of York Beach project manager and a former owner of the Ocean House said the developers are 'preserving it for posterity.' He said he expects some of the units to be ready for occupancy next summer, with preconstruction prices ranging from $130,000 to $200,000.

"'This is one of the most significant projects of its kind in Maine,' said Ocean House marketing director Robert Bowes. 'This is a landmark structure that has been the heart of this town's oceanfront for more than 100 years. We are going to preserve the essential Ocean House image and restore it to the classic luxury it once had. Bowes said he has received more than 100 inquiries from prospective buyers.

"'It's been a long siege,' selectman Arthur Berger told Dunfey while congratulating him on the groundbreaking ceremony. Dunfey, wearing rubbers over his shoes in case of rain, thanked those on hand for coming, despite threatening skies, 'to celebrate the formal start of the Ocean House project.'

"Brennan, who said he once stopped at the Ocean House as a 'Canada Dry delivery person,' stated that the project may be the 'start to a great revitalization project in this area.'"

Demolition

October 2, **The Ocean House is coming down—No surprise to some as York code officer gives demolish order,** by staff writer Pam O'Neil, *Portsmouth Herald*:

"YORK—Once again sands have shifted under the Ocean House.

"One week after Maine's governor celebrated the start of reconstruction here, the old York Beach hotel was condemned as a dangerous building.

"York Code Officer Bob Davis on Tuesday ordered the owners to 'demolish' it 'as soon as practical.'

Advertisement: Announcing advance sales for Ocean House condominiums. (Betsy Camp)

THE CRANES MOVED IN this week to begin removing parts of the roof on the Ocean House hotel in York Beach, in the wake of a demolition order from the town code enforcement officer.   *Photo by Dean Rock*

"'Our plans won't change,' Dunfey said. 'We still intend to save certain portions and reuse as much as possible.'

"Davis said, 'What's going to happen there is exactly what the Planning Board approved.' Local zoning and building codes 'allow for the rebuilding of structures destroyed by fire, acts of God or condemnation.'

"Owner Bob Dunfey of Seabury Housing Associates is not surprised. He said Davis has merely confirmed and put into writing 'what has been known for the last couple of weeks.'

"Both men said the Oct. 1 condemnation order has no effect on Seabury's plans to develop a multimillion-dollar condominium at the Ocean Avenue site.

"Planning Chairman Dave Linney said the matter will be discussed at Thursday night's board meeting.

"Linney questioned how the developers could have remained unaware of the building's dangerous condition. 'I don't understand,' he said. 'They hired a reputable architect. They researched it. I don't know how they could've missed it. . . .'

"Mentioning the 'timing' of the project, Dunfey said as the results of more and more studies came in he said his group realized the job would be more and more expensive.

"'Redefined' plans now call for the façade and the two towers to be carefully removed, and the rest to be taken apart in manageable sections (probably room by room) to see what can be used.

Section of north wing roof being removed by crane. (David Pahl)

"'We're still going to preserve the building's historic character and retain it as a landmark site,' Dunfey said.

October 9, **Board miffed over hotel reconstruction,** by John Breneman, *York Weekly*:

"The proposed reconstruction of the Ocean House in York Beach, a project that was finally approved by the York Planning Board after 15 months of review, was back before the board last Thursday after it became clear that the 120-plus-year-old building must be demolished.

Part of the building façade being lowered to the ground. (David Pahl)

"'The plan was never presented to us as a demolition project,' said planning board chairman David Linney. The other board members agreed with Linney's assertion that the project was never reviewed as 'anything but a rehabilitated building.'

"Acting on a unanimous vote of the board, Town Planner Tony Dater met with town attorney E. Stephen Murray in his Portland office Monday morning with York Code Enforcement Officer Robert Davis, who issued a condemnation order to Seabury Housing Associates, developer of the project, and its president Robert Dunfey Jr. on Oct. 1. "'We don't like surprises. To me, this was a very big surprise,' Linney said of the condemnation order. Former York Code Enforcement Officer Armand Tremblay, who worked with the planning board during its review, said it never dawned on him that the board didn't see the project as a reconstruction.

"Tremblay cited a 'lack of communication' and stated that a plan approved by the state fire marshal 'clearly shows that it's not the same building.'

"'A reconstruction is what the whole thing was,' said Tremblay, adding, 'essentially, as far as the design of the building is concerned

REVIEW — The Ocean House "is the biggest project York has ever seen," said Code Officer Bob Davis, right, as he, Selectman Margaret Dixon, and owner Bob Dunfey pored over architectural drawings of the $5 million-plus condominium development last night, just after the Planning Board enacted a temporarily delay. (Staff photo by O'Neil)

Removal of Ocean House exterior walls, October 9, 1985.
(Museums of Old York)

the appeals board to extend the roofline and lengthen the building, since state statute seems to allow rebuilding a condemned structure to its original footprint.

"With a 53-foot roofline, the original Ocean House was grand fathered with respect to York Beach zoning that allows a maximum height of 35 feet. Dater also sought advice on the validity of the approved plan now that demolition of the building has begun.

"Dater this week said Murray 'is going to put his opinion to those questions in writing' within the next few days, detailing 'procedural options, legal options that everyone has in this matter.'

it will be the same.' A Sept. 20 letter from project architect Warren Freedenfeld stated, 'This undertaking is not and never has been a restoration project, per se.'

"'Everyone wasn't understanding what everyone else was doing,' said Dater. 'I thought it was . . . preserving the grandfathered main structure of Ocean House. I never heard the word demolition.'

"Dater was asked by the board to solicit Murray's legal opinion on 'how would this condemnation affect the grandfathering of the Ocean House and the variance given by

"'We'll just continue rolling,' said Dunfey, adding that the planning board is 'not necessarily trying to hinder the project,' but rather, 'protecting themselves against a precedent.'

"'I'm upset, we've always been working with the town,' said Dunfey. 'I thought I could start construction in June or July' and complete the project, which he expects to cost 'in excess of $5 million,' a year later. Delays, he stated, are costing 'tens of thousands (of dollars) a month.'"

"'This is a magnificent project,' said Dunfey, adding that he and his contractor, Donalco, Inc. of South Portland, are 'going to save as much as we can' of the original building.

"During the meeting, selectmen chairman Michael Palumbo stood and read his memo supporting the Ocean House project. Delaying the reconstruction, he said, is 'beating a dead horse to death a second time.'

Roof of turret being removed from above the dining room porch.
(David Pahl)

"'We had all hoped to save the Ocean House, but the facts at this time do not dictate that option,' Palumbo stated, adding that 'the new building will be a far better end product and a first-class project.'

"'Nowhere does it mention on the approved Mylar the words 'restoration,'" noted Palumbo, who submitted that, as long as the developers build what is on the plan signed by the board, the planning board and the town planner have 'no further jurisdiction.'

"'I believe this good project will be a catalyst for the revitalization of York Beach. Let's not put any further roadblocks in its path,' Palumbo concluded.

"'What is going to be there next year will have the same visual impact' as what is called for on the approved plan, according to Davis who made a difficult decision in favor of condemnation.

"After inspecting the structure and finding support posts that have been 'in a state of decay for an extremely long time' and support beams that were 'cut and never rebraced,' Davis concluded that, 'attempts to move the structure would create a hazard to the workers and those in the vicinity.'

"'If you smoked a cigarette in the basement today, you would smell it in the attic in minutes,' Davis said, illustrating some of the danger.

"I don't know why this (the need for demolition) didn't come to light earlier. This miffs me a little bit,' said Linney, who added that Freedenfeld should have been aware of the building's condition.

Rear view of the main building debris being carted away, York Manor is at right. (David Pahl)

"'It's part of an architect's job. They're schooled in that sort of thing,' Linney said. 'We should have all the facts in front of us' when reviewing a project, he said.

"'I feel we were misled,' said board member Nancy Rohrer, who had earlier stated, 'In good faith we reviewed them as a restoration of a building' and 'approved a plan for a restoration of an existing building.'

"Linney agreed the plan was 'approved under the planning board's feeling that it was a renovation' and said he was unsure 'where the plan stands at this point,' but will wait for Murray's opinion.

Pile driving foundation supports, looking through the site toward York Manor. (David Pahl)

Main building construction and town house footings. (David Pahl)

conversion and additions is also temporarily void.

"All parties agreed, however, that foundation work could continue at the site, located on Ocean Avenue across from Short Sands in York Beach.

"To get back on track, Seabury will have to secure at least a height-variance from the Appeals board.

"Since the board recently reconfirmed permission for a roof-line extension 52 feet high, Seabury President Bob Dunfey sees no problem there.

"The Planning Board based its decision on an opinion from Town Attorney Steve Murray.

"Basically Murray advised that once a building is demolished (as the Ocean House now is), it loses its grandfathered rights under local zoning which permits 'maintenance, repair, and improvement of nonconforming structures.'

"Determining that a brand new building will not have those rights, the Planning Board acted in an effort to comply with the law and to avoid setting a loose precedent.

"'Everyone thinks the project is a good one which will be a boon to York Beach's revitalization,' planning member Nancy Rohrer told Dunfey.

"'I'm here to put this issue to rest,' said Dunfey, who, now it seems, will have to wait to 'put the dead horse in its grave.'"

October 18, **Ocean House plans suspended,** by staff writer Pam O'Neil, *Portsmouth Herald*:

"YORK—For a short while anyway, the Ocean House project has gone adrift.

"The Planning Board last night suspended its approval of plans for the site until required variances are obtained.

"This means the building permit held by owner Seabury Associates for condominium

Cavanaugh cottage at left, town house site, and main building construction. (David Pahl)

"'We're not trying to put a stumbling block in the way. We just want to go by the book.'

"Board Chairman Dave Linney echoed her comments, saying 'We all want to see this thing built . . . but there are some very serious considerations here, which I think the Appeals Board should consider too.'

"If approval were not revoked, it could 'open the door to all the old houses in town.'

"Linney was still angry about one point. It 'really yanks me off that the board didn't know the building was going to be demolished.' And that the former code officer apparently knew all along but thought it was none of the board's business. Dunfey said he didn't know himself until September.

"And Linney responded, then 'I think the people you hired were negligent.'

"Along with notification of their vote, the planning members will send the Appeals Board a memo on grandfathering rights and other points on which their decision was based.

"Now 'the ball's in their court,' Linney said.

"GAG

"The Planners also voted to meet with the selectmen on Oct. 29 to discuss the order silencing Town Planner Tony Dater on the Ocean House project.

"Particularly disturbed by the selectmen's action, Mrs. Rohrer indicated this time they have pushed the board too far."

Construction progress on the main building in March 1986. (Betsy Camp)

October 23, "SEABURY HOUSING ASSO-CIATES, a Maine corporation of Portland, County of Cumberland and State of Maine for consideration paid, release to THE INHABITANTS OF THE TOWN OF YORK, County of York and State of Maine

"A use easement on a certain lot or parcel of land situated at York Beach, in the Town and County of York and State of Maine lying on the northerly side of U.S. Route 1-A known as Ocean Avenue directly lying in front of the "Ocean House" one hundred (100) feet square to be used in connection with the Ocean House for a pleasure ground.

The Pleasure Ground in front of Ocean House c. 1900. (Author's collection)

"Said tract is further described as, Another lot of land one hundred (100) feet square, with a paved walk leading thereto and to the Sea, situated on the northeasterly side of said Ocean Avenue, lying wholly within the area of land comprising the 'Park', and directly in front of said Hotel, said lot being used in connection with said Hotel for a 'Pleasure Ground', which said lot was reserved to Ellen N. Ellis in the deed from Ellen N. Ellis et al., to Carlos B. Mosley et al., dated August 15, 1887, and recorded in the York County Registry of Deeds, [418/34]

"Being a portion of the premises conveyed to Seabury Housing Associates by Orbust, Inc. by deed dated May 29, 1985 and recorded in York County Registry of Deeds. [3533/174]

"Reference is hereby made to the Decree of the York County Superior Court, dated December 4, 1968 in the case of Ocean House, Inc. versus James Peck et al., Civil Action Docket No. 9456 and to the Plan of Property in York Beach, Maine made for Ellis Park by H. I. & E. C. Jordan, dated August 1983 and recorded in the York County Registry of Deeds. [Plan 125/12]

"This release is given subject to the conditions that no buildings or structures of any kind shall be erected on said 100 square foot area, and that no trees or shrubs of a height greater than 10 feet shall be planted or placed within said area. [3802/89]

"Meaning and intending to convey and release only the premises and rights described under the caption Easement B in the deed to Seabury Housing Associates from Orbust, Inc., dated May 29, 1985 and recorded in said Registry of Deeds." [3533/174]

1986

January 14, Seabury Housing Associates granted a mortgage to Maine Savings Bank in the amount of $9,355,745.00 plus interest and other charges as provided in the mortgage. [3738/177] The bank agreed to release individual units from the Mortgage and Security Agreement upon sale by Seabury in exchange for the net sale proceeds.

Fire!

May 20, **Ocean House destroyed,** by staff writer Neil Cote, *Portsmouth Herald:*

"YORK—The rebuilding of Ocean House suffered a serious setback early this morning as a fire of undetermined origin swept through the Short Sands Beach construction site, destroying the wood frame structure and much of the foundation.

"'It looked like the Fourth of July.' Fire Chief John Welch remarked shortly after the crack of dawn while firefighters continued to spray water on still-smoldering timbers.

THE OCEAN HOUSE *as it looked one week before the blaze destroyed all but a small section of turret in the south end of the property on May 20.* THE YORK WEEKLY • MAY 28, 1986. *Photo by Dean Rock*

Photo by Dean Rock: From the May 28, 1986 York Weekly article by John Breneman entitled "Cause of Ocean House fire called 'Suspicious.'" (Betsy Camp)

Rear of the main building with Cavanaugh cottage at left. (David Pahl)

'Everything was lit up. In a matter of minutes it (the flames) went from one end of the building to the other.'

"The state's chief fire investigator, Maine Fire Marshal Donald Bissette, was expected to arrive at the scene later today. Welch would not speculate when asked how the blaze may have originated.

"Robert Dunfey, president of Seabury Housing Associates, the firm rebuilding the Ocean House, said it was too early to say how far back the anticipated completion date has

Rear of main building with upper floors collapsed (David Pahl)

A hose is directed at the burning Ocean House about 4:30 a.m. shortly after firefighters arrived on scene. It went up very quickly, leaving little time for York Beach and York Village volunteers to try and save it.

Staff photographs by Dan Gair

"A fire destroyed the Ocean House at York Beach in a matter of minutes early Tuesday morning, doing more that $1 million in damage to the partially completed structure.

"Fifty firefighters from the York Beach and York Village fire departments worked for an hour and a half to contain the blaze, which started about 4 a.m. They prevented neighboring houses from catching on fire, and no injuries occurred.

"State Fire Marshal Joe Levasseur was at the site until 10 p.m. Tuesday, but had not determined the cause of the fire by this morning. Levasseur said the fire started in the central portion of the building but a lot of debris must be removed before he can get to the source.

"Levasseur said he has not ruled out any possible origin, including arson.

"Developer Robert Dunfey, who was modeling his Ocean House condominium project after a 127-year-old hotel that stood on the same site until torn down last year, said he will start rebuilding as soon as possible.

"'We're going to clean up and just charge along,' he said Tuesday morning.

"The exterior of the four-story building, which is to be an exact replica of the former hotel, was almost complete and builders were preparing to put on the roof. On the inside, studding, some duct work and some

been pushed. Seabury had hoped to complete the project by the end of the summer.

"'We have to investigate what caused the fire and speak to our insurance agents,' was all Dunfey would say this morning.

"Welch said his department was notified of the fire shortly before 4 a.m., and that the flames rapidly consumed the wooden framework. The blaze apparently began in the southwest corner of the building, according to Welch, and swept across the entire structure in just several minutes.

"Firefighters battled the flames with water, and sprayed several area houses as well to minimize the chances of the fire spreading to adjacent buildings.

"At least one house sustained minor water damage, and Welsh commented that the densely-built beach area was lucky that most of the fire was confined to the Ocean House . . ."

May 21, **Fire consumes Ocean House; developer vows he will rebuild,** by Shannon Brennan, *York County Coast Star:*

---

plumbing and electrical work had been done, Dunfey said, noting that the electricity is turned off at the end of each work day.

"Dunfey emphasized that the reason the building burned so quickly is because no fire walls or sprinkling systems had been installed. Only a small amount of framing on the south end survived the fire, but it will have to be knocked down. The concrete foundation, however, should not have to be replaced, he said.

"Although the building was insured, Dunfey said he expects the fire to cost him more that the insurance company will reimburse him. He estimated the damage at more than $1 million.

"All 43 condominium units in the structure, along with the 23 units in townhouses that have not been built have been sold for between $129,000 and $229,000. Dunfey had hoped to complete the project by late fall, but said he cannot predict when it will be finished now.

"Dunfey said he is sending notices to all buyers to let them know about the fire and the delay it will cause.

"Both Dunfey and neighbors of the project had nothing but praise for the firefighters. Although the York Beach station is just around the corner from the Ocean House, firefighters could do nothing to save it.

"York Beach Fire Chief John Welch said the structure was already engulfed in flames when they arrived so they

At daybreak, construction scaffolding stands out against smoke-filled sky as remains burn. The melted steel girders that once held second floor are an indication of fire's intensity. Officials say nearby homeowners were lucky wind was blowing out to sea.

concentrated on saving Tom Cavanaugh's house.

"'They did a fabulous job,' Cavanaugh said. 'We're very fortunate.' Cavanaugh's house, which sits immediately north of the Ocean House, had only minor damage considering its proximity to the blaze. Sections of the roof will have to be replaced and some damage

Firefighters survey smouldering ruins of York Beach's Ocean House project atop the first floor's foundation. Toppled sign burns below during actual fire hours earlier.

Fire trucks pouring water on the Cavanaugh cottage (David Pahl) Volunteer firefighter Phil Meader was laying on his back on the Ocean House side of the Cavanaugh's directing water at their house while another firefighter sprayed water on Phil to keep him from getting burned. (2014 conversation with Phil Meader)

was done to the south side of the house from the water poured on it to keep it from igniting.

"'I never saw a fire move so fast,' Cavanaugh said.

"He and his wife, Nancy were awakened by the alarm at the fire station. They looked out at the ball field behind their house and saw lights. When they heard crackling sounds, they realized a fire was next door.

"Volunteer firefighter Mark Gay said his truck was the first on the scene. Gay said it took about two to three minutes for the building to be consumed in flames and another two to three to collapse.

"'All the water in the world could not have stopped it,' he said.

"No one expected the new building to burn, after years of worrying that the old hotel would catch on fire. 'We waited for years for that thing to go,' Gay said.

"Neighbors on the south end of the Ocean House made the same comment. Ken and Barbara Perry, who own the York Manor Apartments, said they had worried that the old hotel was a fire trap.

"'We've always said that if that goes up, we better hope the wind is blowing right.' Barbara Perry said.

"For the Perrys, the wind was blowing right Tuesday. The vinyl siding on the north side of their apartment building will have to be replaced because of heat damage, but the wind blew the flames away from their house.

"Back on the other side of the Ocean House, Beverly and Larry Bowen were saying thanks that Cavanaugh's house did not go up. The Sands Motel, which they manage, was next in line.

Fire investigators on the scene. (Museums of Old York)

"Beverly Bowen said the crackling fire woke them up and her husband called the fire station. She said they did not have to evacuate the 15 guests that were in the motel, but kept a close eye on the Cavanaugh dwelling.

"Larry Bowen, who has been taking pictures of the progress of the Ocean House construction, has pictures of the fire to add to his collection. But he also will have reconstruction photos soon.

"Although Dunfey was optimistic about putting the pieces back together, he said the fire was terribly discouraging. One of the subcontractors broke out in tears when he saw the destruction.

"'They put so much of themselves into it,' Dunfey said."

Rebuilding

Seabury Housing Associates created a brochure promoting "The Ocean House, a Condominium Residence at York Beach." The text from page 1 follows:

"The elegance of a bygone era is now a dream come true!

"The last of many grand hotels that once dotted the coast of Southern Maine, The Ocean House was built in 1862 as The Ocean Wave Roller Skating Pavilion. [There may have been another building in downtown York Beach by this name; the date is certainly incorrect.] At that time, it was described, 'as being situated on an elevation on Short Sands Beach, (and) always favored with a cool sea-breeze which rendered refreshment at all times.'

"For more than a century and a quarter, generations of summer visitors and year round residents have come to associate the grandeur of The Ocean House—its gracious verandas, stately towers and sweeping roofline—with the best memories of vacationing at Short Sands in York Beach, Maine.

"The original building, along with an architecturally elegant three story addition, was established as a grand hotel in 1884 [the addition came later]; where guests always dressed for dinner and were

The fire scene from Ellis Short Sands Park. (David Pahl)

Ocean House veranda, c. 1942. (Author's collection)

served by waiters and chambermaids in crisp white uniforms.

"Today, The Ocean House more than symbolizes the grace and elegance of a bygone era. The reconstruction of The Ocean House Condominiums at York Beach mirrors not only the original building, but the spirit of The Ocean House itself.

"An invitation to join in the spirit of The Ocean House and to enjoy a luxury year round home cordially awaits you."

September 3, **Condominiums delayed by fire going back up,** by Shannon Brennan, *York County Coast Star*:

"The Ocean House condominium project at York Beach will not be finished until late spring or early summer of 1987, developer Robert Dunfey said Tuesday during a post-Labor Day ceremony to thank his construction workers for 'hanging in there.'

"Dunfey was in the process of building a replica of the old Ocean House hotel that had graced Short Sands Beach for 127 years when a May 20 fire destroyed it. Police are still looking for the persons who set the fire.

"Until last week, passersby had seen little progress on the main building that had been destroyed by fire. The delay was caused by a disagreement between Dunfey's contractor and his insurance company about how to repair the surface of the foundation. Now, the first floor is going back up.

"Work has progressed all summer, however, on the townhouses being built behind the central building. The $5 million project will include 43 units in the main, four-story building and 23 units in the townhouses.

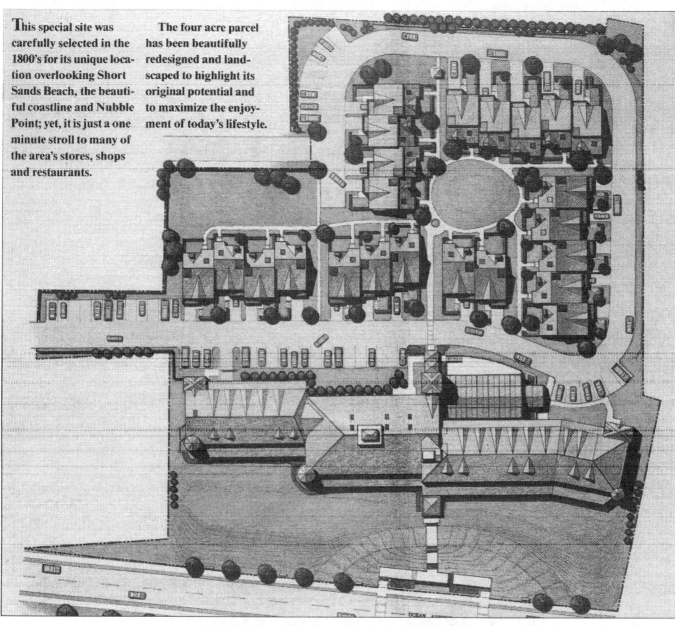

This special site was carefully selected in the 1800's for its unique location overlooking Short Sands Beach, the beautiful coastline and Nubble Point; yet, it is just a one minute stroll to many of the area's stores, shops and restaurants.

The four acre parcel has been beautifully redesigned and landscaped to highlight its original potential and to maximize the enjoyment of today's lifestyle.

Page 3 of the Seabury Housing Associates brochure.

"All but two of the units have been sold, and Dunfey said buyers are still committed to purchasing their units. The units sold for between $129,000 and $229,000.

"On Tuesday morning, Dunfey provided coffee, doughnuts and T-shirts to the construction crew members to thank them for their double efforts. 'We set this up to thank you for hanging in there since the fire last May,' he said.

"Allen Folsom, job foreman for Keefe Construction, said he took the fire in stride. 'If we weren't working here, we'd be on another one. It's not easier the second time, but we've done it once so it should go a lot quicker.'

"Folsom said only five of his original crew is still working on the Ocean House, however, so most of his 16 workers are new on the job. The hardest part of the job is the commute most of them have. Folsom drives from

Staff photograph by Shannon Brennan

Work progresses on the Ocean House at York Beach, the controversial condominium project that was set on fire in May. Police are still looking for the person or persons responsible for the blaze.

North Windham every day and another 10 men drive from Portland, he said.

"Folsom said his crew should have all the buildings enclosed by December, when their work will end."

1988

July 15, **Penalty imposed for discharging fill behind the Ocean House,** *Biddeford Journal*:

Ocean House rebuilding progress in December 1986. (Museums of Old York)

"August 13, 1988 Action: Notice of Proposed Penalty Order and Opportunity to Comment. The Environmental Protection Agency (EPA), Region I, is providing notice of and opportunity to comment on a proposed Class I Administrative Penalty, in the amount of $18,000, to be assessed against Seabury Housing Associates of Portland, Maine. Seabury Housing Associates discharged fill material into wetlands without the proper federal authorization to construct a portion of their Ocean House Condominium project located in York Beach, Maine. By discharging fill material into wetlands without the proper federal authorization, Seabury Housing Associates violated section 301 of the Clean Water Act (Act). Section 309(g) of the Act authorizes EPA to issue orders assessing civil administrative penalties for various violations of the Act. EPA may issue such orders after the commencement of a Class I penalty proceeding."

September 15, In Civil Court Case Number 87-0350-P (Archived on the website leagle.com) Seabury Housing Associates, Plaintiff, filed a lawsuit to recover fire

Wetlands filled in for Town House construction behind the Ocean House.
(David Pahl)

related costs from the Home Insurance Company and Dunfey Agency, Inc., Defendants:

"I. Introduction

"During the construction of a condominium project in York, Maine, Plaintiff Seabury Housing Associates ('Seabury') engaged Dunfey Agency ('Dunfey') to secure insurance for the project. With Seabury's consent, Dunfey selected a builder's risk policy offered by The Home Insurance Company ('Home'), and completed the necessary documentation. Dunfey then assured Seabury that the project was comprehensively insured.

"Approximately three months after the policy took effect Seabury's condominium project was destroyed by fire. Seabury filed, and Home paid, two claims for damages and costs. A year later, Seabury filed a claim for 'soft costs.' Home refused to pay the claim, arguing that Seabury's policy did not provide 'soft costs coverage.'

"Seabury filed this action against Dunfey and Home, alleging that Home breached the insurance policy, violated Maine law by disputing an insurance claim in bad faith, and breached its duty of good faith and fair dealing. Seabury claims that if its policy did not contain soft costs coverage, then Dunfey had breached its agreement to secure the coverage Seabury had requested, had negligently failed to obtain the proper coverage, had negligently misrepresented the scope of Seabury's coverage, and had breached its fiduciary duty to Seabury.

"Home filed a cross-claim against Dunfey for contribution and indemnification. Dunfey, in turn, filed a similar cross-claim against Home. Seabury has moved for partial summary judgment against Home on the issue of liability. Home has itself moved for summary judgment against Seabury and Dunfey, claiming that the policy unambiguously excludes soft costs coverage, [695 F. Supp. 1246] and claiming that Seabury has not introduced sufficient evidence of bad faith to support an action under 24-A M.R.S.A. § 2436 or a claim for punitive damages.

"For reasons set forth in this opinion, the Court denies Plaintiff's motion, grants Home's motion as to the bad faith, and denies Home's motion in all other respects . . ."

1990

January 5, Parking garage spaces were reallocated as follows: Unit 303 has no space; Unit 311 has space #11; Unit 214 has space #12; Unit 211 has space #15. Document signed by Robert J. Dunfey Jr. as president of Seabury Housing Associates. [5299/185]

November 28, A foreclosure sale of five Ocean House Condominium Units to be held on Dec 1, 1990 was announced in the *York County Coast-Star.* The units to be sold

Ocean House main building as completed by Seabury Housing Associates in 1990. (by Author, 2007)

were 211, 303, 305, A-4 and E-3. Three units had already been partially released from the subject mortgage: Unit 214 on April 6, 1990; [5362/324] Unit 311 on February 7, 1990; [5317/239] and Unit 314 on April 6, 1990. [5363/48]

Epilogue

December 1, 1990, The public sale was held, as described in the public notice, at the Ocean House. All remaining mortgaged premises were sold at this time to the highest bidders for an amount less than the outstanding balance of the mortgage. [5586/127]

This ended Seabury Housing Associates involvement with Ocean House, and responsibility for management of the property now fell to the Ocean House Condominium Association and its elected board of directors.

December 10, 1993, **President Names Dunfey to GSA Regional Post,** White House, Office of the Press Secretary:

"President Clinton announced today that he has appointed Maine businessman Robert J. Dunfey Jr. to be the Deputy Regional Administrator of the General Services Administration for Regions I and II, covering the Northeastern part of the country.

"Dunfey joins the General Services Administration from the international trade business, where he has been serving as an agent primarily involved with U.S. exports to Asia and joint ventures between U.S. interests and Asian businesses. Prior to 1992, Mr. Dunfey was with Quality Suites Hotel in Portland, Maine where he was the managing partner and executive director for three years. In that capacity, he developed, sought approvals from federal, state and local authorities, financed, constructed, opened and operated Portland's first all-suites and airport hotel. Prior to his experience with Quality Suites Hotel, Mr. Dunfey was the president and general partner of Dunfey Properties from 1985 to 1990 . . . "

CHAPTER 5

Ocean House Condominium Association

1986

March 1, The first article in the Declaration of Condominium describes the legal basis for the creation of the Ocean House Condominium Association and the second article describes its responsibilities:

ARTICLE I: GENERAL PROVISIONS AND APPLICABILITY

The Ocean House, a Condominium Residence was created by a Declaration of Condominium for The Ocean House, A Condominium Residence, dated March 1, 1986 and recorded in the York County Registry of Deeds pursuant to the Maine Condominium Act, Chapter 31 of Title 33, Maine Revised Statutes of 1964, as amended. In accordance with the requirements of the Act, The Ocean House Condominium Association was organized as a non-profit corporation under the Maine Non-profit Corporation Act, Title 13-B of the Maine Revised Statutes of 1964, as amended. Pursuant to the Act, every Unit Owner and all persons entitled to occupy a Unit shall comply with these Bylaws of the Association . . . The office of the Condominium, the Association and the Executive Board shall be located at the condominium or at such other place as may be designated by the Executive Board from time to time.

ARTICLE II: POWERS OF ASSOCIATION

"The Association is the governing body for all of the Unit Owners with respect to the administration, maintenance, repair, replacement, cleaning, sanitation, management and operation of the Common Elements and of certain other matters. Subject to the provisions of the Declaration, the Association may:

The Ocean House, a Condominium Residence, February 25, 2007. (by Author)

- Adopt and amend bylaws and rules and regulations for the operation of the Association and the Condominium;

- Adopt and amend budgets for revenues, expenditures and reserves and collect assessments for common expenses from unit owners;

Ocean House pool, February 25, 2007. (by Author)

- Hire and terminate managing agents and other employees, agents and independent contractors;

- Institute, defend or intervene in litigation or administrative proceedings in its own name on behalf of itself or 2 or more unit owners on matters affecting the Condominium;

- Make contracts and incur liabilities;

- Regulate the use, maintenance, repair, replacement and modification of common elements;

- Cause additional improvements to be made as part of the Common Elements;

- Acquire, hold, encumber and convey in its own name any right, title or interest or real or personal property, provided that common elements may be conveyed or subjected to a security interest only pursuant to Section 1603-112 of the Condominium Act and subject to the prior approval of Eligible Mortgage Holders as provided in the Declaration;

- Grant easements, leases, licenses and concessions through or over the common elements;

- Impose and receive any payments, fees or charges for the use, rental or operation of the common elements, other than limited common elements described in Section 1602-102 of the Condominium Act, and for services provided to unit owners:

York Beach businesses weathered the storm this past weekend, with many business owners battening down the hatches and staying on board at their establishments to assess the damage as rising waters meant for stranded cars, floating dumpsters and propane tanks and stranded patrons. *Photo by Paul R. Ladd, III*

- Impose charges for late payment of assessments and, after notice and an opportunity to be heard, levy reasonable fines for violations of the Declaration, bylaws and rules and regulations of the association;

- Impose reasonable charges of the preparation and recordation of amendments to the Declaration, resale certificates required by the Condominium Act or statements of unpaid assessments;

- Provide for the indemnification of its officers and Executive Board and maintain directors' and officers' liability insurance;

- Assign its right to future income including the right to receive common expense assessments, but only to the extent the Declaration or these Bylaws as incorporated therein expressly so provide;

- Exercise any other powers conferred by the Declaration or bylaws;

- Exercise all other powers that may be exercised in this State by legal entities of the same type as the Association or as authorized by the Act; and

- Exercise any other powers necessary or proper for the governance and operation of the Association . . ."

2006

May 17, **Weathering the storm . . .,** *Independent Voice of the Yorks and Ogunquit:*

"Between Saturday, May 13, and [Wednesday, May 17], over 13 inches of rain has fallen on southern York County, at times creating a deluge over both York and Ogunquit.

"York Emergency Management Director and Police Chief Douglas Bracy has described the ensuing surge of water to Short Sands, Long Sands and through local rivers and roadways a '500-year flood' based on the magnitude of the damage it has wrought.

"And, town officials warn, the flooding was due to fresh water alone—not the ocean . . ."

Damage to the Ocean House condominiums was limited to a few inches of water in the basement storage lockers and maintenance required to dry out equipment in the elevator shaft.

Capital Improvement Program (CIP)

2007

May 26, After 20 years of being exposed to the high winds, rain, and salt air prevalent at the ocean, chronic leaks in the Ocean House exterior were an ever increasing drain on the

---

budget. At the annual meeting of the Ocean House Condominium Association, the board of directors made a strong case for a comprehensive capital improvement program.

According to the meeting minutes, a motion was made to "Approve the full CIP, as presented this date of May 26, 2007 at the Annual Meeting of the Membership and thereby authorize the BOD (Board of Directors) to obtain an Association Loan for 4.1 Million Dollars." This motion failed with 42 percent in favor and 31 percent against (50 percent was required).

Another motion was made to "Approve the full CIP, as presented this date of May 26, 2007 at the Annual Meeting of the Membership and thereby authorize the BOD to make an Assessment up to 4.1 Million Dollars. Assessments will be levied to the owners based on the contractual payment schedules. Owners will be assessed according to the percentage of ownership." This motion passed with 54 percent in favor and 26 percent opposed.

August 25, Ames Associates LLC, an engineering and architectural company, completed plans and specifications and held a pre-bid meeting and site walk for seven contractors. Selection of a successful bidder was held off pending a special meeting of the Ocean House Condominium Association in September.

September 29, At the special meeting, Brian Ames of Ames Associates LLC made his recommendation that contractor Schernecker Property Services (SPS) be awarded the CIP contract, based on bid pricing, specialization to condominium projects, level of qualifications and experience, and background checks. Presentations were also made by Ocean House legal counsel and a loan officer from Community Association Banc (division of Mutual of Omaha). After all questions were answered, a motion was made to authorize the board to borrow up to $3.4 million to fund the CIP approved at the 2007 Annual Meeting. Options for owner payment by lump sum or a loan program were included. The vote by show of hands plus proxy was 97 percent in favor, no opposition present; motion passed unanimously.

Contractor SPS had the work substantially completed by April 2009.

2008–2009

In their newsletter, Schernecker Property Services showcased the 'CIP' project at Ocean House:

"Fall 2009—Customer Focus—SPS Turns the Tide at Ocean House

Town house exterior construction on February 2, 2008. (by Author)

"At Ocean House Condominiums in York, Maine, the ocean views are spectacular. But the forces of nature have not been kind to the building envelope. Aging roofs, cedar shingles, and pine trim were no match for the power of wind-driven rain. And repairs had become increasingly expensive and ineffective.

"'Patchwork fixes only get you so far,' says Association President Gabe Vellante. 'We needed a full engineering study and a plan.'

"Built in 1986, the Ocean House complex

Upper level work above the pool, May 6, 2008. (by Author)

consists of 43 luxury units in the main building—a grand 4-story structure reputed to be one of the largest wooden frame buildings in the United States—and 23 town house units in separate buildings.

"The engineer's report called for a multi-million dollar envelope makeover. Vellante, a building commissioner, knew the association needed a contractor with the experience, expertise and resources to handle complex, large-scale projects. After a competitive bidding process, the Board hired Schernecker Property Services.

"'This was a huge job, and the devil was in the details,' says Vellante, who also cites SPS's longevity and reputation for standing behind their work as factors in the Board's decision. 'What good is a warranty if the contractor isn't around to honor it?'

"SPS crews stripped and replaced the roofs and siding, repairing rotted sheathing and framing as necessary. Extra attention was paid to flashing details and proper installation of the new siding system—Certainteed Cedar Impressions vinyl shingles backed by a VaproShield wind and moisture barrier. All pine trim was replaced with new PVC trim.

Heat pump bump-outs and catwalks on rear of main building May 6, 2008. (by Author)

Front of the main building, November 2, 2008. (by Author)

"Whenever possible, instead of using J-channel around windows, siding was terminated behind rabbit-cut PVC trim fastened with stainless steel screws. 'We wanted to be able to replace windows without having to take the siding apart,' says Vellante. 'It also looks a lot better.'

"All 43 pocket decks on the main building were renovated with new PVC decking, PVC railing systems, custom-made PVC lattice work, and wooden 3-panel French doors. New sliding doors were also installed in each townhouse unit.

"Vellante credits SPS's project management team for bringing the challenging project in on time and on budget, noting that SPS Business Manager Jeff Pike and COO Brian Brown impressed the Board at weekly production meetings. 'Architectural plans always look good on paper,' says Vellante. 'But when we encountered gaps between the drawings and real-world application, SPS's management team often came up with alternative solutions. And if a problem was SPS's

Front entry of the main building near the end of the project, April 27, 2009. (by Author)

Exterior reconstruction completed, May 10, 2009. (by Author)

responsibility, they always stepped up and did the right thing.'

"SPS's Brian Brown attributes a large part of the project's success to the Ocean House Board of Directors. 'The Association was fortunate to have a team of construction and financial professionals who really knew their stuff,' says Brown. "The result is a beautiful oceanfront property with a low-maintenance envelope that can stand up to the elements and looks great year round . . ."

Conclusion

Hopefully this book will satisfy the curiosity of all who have passed by the Ocean House and wondered what that imposing gray castle-like structure is and how it came to be at the epicenter of Short Sands Beach. It is intended to be a historical record for the ages. As time passes few people know about the key role the Ellis family played in developing sandy scrub land into a family resort community called York Beach; fond memories of former guests and employees fade into the distance; and the only evidence that a hotel once existed is found on postcards being sold on eBay. The author hopes you enjoy reading this book as much as he enjoyed discovering the true past of Ocean House in York Beach, Maine.